The Returning Ones

A Medium's Memoirs

SHIRL KNOBLOCH

The Returning Ones: A Medium's Memoirs

© Shirley Knobloch, 2013

ISBN 13: 978-0-9885171-2-7

Edited by: Jennifer Sabatelli

Cover photo by: Rebecca Norberg

The author is pictured wearing an authentic 19th century wedding dress, holding a 19th century daguerreotype, both from her personal collection of Civil War Era antiques.

Also by Shirl Knobloch:

Birdsong, Barks, and Banter: Adventures of an Animal Intuitive Reiki Master and Her Home of Misfit Companions
(Available on Amazon.com)

Dedicated to JBee, my friend

Table of Contents

Prologue   1

Where We Left Off...   2

Part One: The Beginnings

Beginning This Journey   12

What Is a Ghost?   14

Being Drawn to Haunted Places   16

Grain House   17

Why Grain House Is So Haunted   19

My First Visitor   21

The Perfect Storm   22

One Man's Poison Is Another Mouse's Candy Cane   27

City Girl/Country Mice   29

Part Two: Moves with Intention

The Whispers of Ghosts   32

You Never Have a Camera Ready   36

Blood-Stained Quilt   38

Blood-Splattered Floor   39

General Lee's A-Coming   41

The Winds of Gettysburg   42

My Farmhouse Table   43

Perfect Time   44

Tidy Ghosts   46

I Think My Mice Are Druids   48

Forget-Me-Nots   50

Mice Humor   52

Tricksters   54

Ghosts Have Ears   56

Sometimes You Have to Accept the Unexplained   58

Don't Make a Ghost Angry   60

Not All Pranksters Are Ghosts   62

Part Three: Hauntings on Hallowed Grounds

Mark Nesbitt's Ghosts of Gettysburg Building   66

The Tillie Pierce House   67

Séance at the Farnsworth House   71

Wandering Spirits   74

Haunting In and About Town   77

Part Four: Spirit Energy

Sparky   84

Sending Spirits to the Light   86

Dark Energy   89

Do Some Humans Carry Dark Energy?   91

Part Five: Past Lives

Glimpses of My Past   96

My Earliest Past   101

A Voice from the Tower   107

Unforgettable Regressions   109

Your Past Will Find You   111

Gazing into Familiar Eyes   113

The Woman in the Picture   116

My Husband's Daguerreotype   119

Gettysburg in the Blood   120

Part Six: Angels

A Good Friday Angel   122

You Never Know When an Angel Is Passing By   126

Sometimes, Spirits Warn   128

Part Seven: Cemeteries

Are Cemeteries Haunted?   132

Green-wood Cemetery: Listening to the Living and the Dead   134

The Cemetery Is Just Like Any Other Neighborhood   137

Part Eight: Paranormal Photographs from Around the World

Caroline   142

Casper at the Grove   143

Dobbin House Anomaly   144

The Reaper Tree   146

The Keyhole Tree   147

The Crucifixion Tree   148

Light Anomalies and Orbs   149

Spirit Animals and Totems   151

My Personal Paranormal Photography Gallery   154

Part Nine: Messages from the Dead

A Visit from My Mother   160

A Little Yellow Bird   162

A Face in the Curtains   164

My Dad's Hello Each Morning   166

A Rose for My Dad   171

Purple Flowers   172

The Old Ones Were Wise   173

Part Ten: The Magick of Ireland

Spirit Stone   178

The Bone of Sligo Abbey   182

Leprechaun's Chair   187

Ghost Box   188

Respect for the Spirits   191

Part Eleven: Goodbye to a Friend

A Heroine's Poppy   196

Part Twelve: From a Place of War to a Place of Wonder

This Magical Place   200

Rainbows on Both Sides of the World   203

Watching a Butterfly Fall Asleep   204

My Work with Animals   206

A Comforting Goodbye   208

Epilogue   210

Native American legend tells of two wolves that walk at our side. One is the white wolf of blessings, joys, happiness, and light. The other is the black wolf of grief, sorrows, despair, and dark.

It is the black wolf that guides us in searching for the mysterious, the unknown, the paranormal. Join me and my spirit totem wolf on a journey to seek out the dark. It is here that we find the most profound faith and enlightenment in life.

Prologue

Remember the vintage television show *Green Acres*? Well, sometimes I feel just like Eva Gabor. Sometimes, in the quietness of Gettysburg's rolling hills, you can hear a scream ring out. Not the cry of a soldier's wandering spirit, but the cry of a city girl encountering some country critter who gets the crazy idea in its mind to come say hello.

Maybe it's the Reiki energy; my house lures every critter like a moth to a flame.

My husband, the hiker and rattlesnake handler (albeit dead ones found on the trail), laughs and thinks it's quite comical.

I don't always laugh.

Sometimes I do.

I hope this book brings some smiles to your face, too, and perhaps some profound introspection about our connection with the Spiritual Realm.

So come along on this city girl's journey into the "wilderness" of Gettysburg, the fairy fields of Ireland, the tortured towers of London, and beyond...and meet some mice and ghosts along the way.

Where We Left Off...

For those of you who have read my first book, *Birdsong, Barks, and Banter*, I wanted to pick up where we left off in this beginning chapter.

My Apache Tears left me only a few short weeks after my book was published. She had spinal cancer, which had spread into her leg and grown rapidly.

After her death, I blogged about her passing. I wish to include those blogs and a poem I wrote to mourn her absence.

"A Goodbye Daisy"

Last night was long and sleepless. This morning, making my way downstairs in the dark was a difficult journey.

One less face was waiting...

One less mouth awaiting breakfast...

My Apache Tears died yesterday. Those of you who have read my book will know her story. She was an eight-year-old sheltie. Spinal cancer took her away from me.

I have seen death over and over. Those who rescue old, sick dogs know it well. But you never know death; sometimes, he surprises you...

The medical profession and the metaphysical world argue over death. Is the tunnel of light simply a misfiring of the brain shutting down and nerve connections breaking down?

I once volunteered at a nursing home for those with Alzheimer's disease. To this day, I remember the screams of those waiting to die, alone in their own little worlds.

I sat with my Apache as she died...she screamed.

The veterinary world explains those screams as the brain's misfiring, as well. Not me. Not if you have heard them.

This morning, in the darkness, I fumbled for my hallway light switch. There, on the floor, was one purple daisy, which had made her descent from a spring wreath of mixed flowers and butterflies that hangs on my pantry door.

Purple was Apache's color—purple collar, purple food bowl, purple leash (though she never used it).

I like to think my girl was waiting for me this morning— waiting to say, "Hello, Mom, I'm ready for breakfast."

It all depends on what you wish to see and hear.

Some see tunnels to journey to the next dimension or the Rainbow Bridge where loved ones wait...

Some see brain malfunctions...

Some hear dying brains...

Some hear screams...

Some see a fallen flower on the floor…

Some see a goodbye daisy.

The Native American legend is true—whoever holds Apache Tears in the palm of her hand will never weep. My palm feels a little emptier now, and I weep for what is gone.

I wrote this blog and poem the second night after Apache Tears left.

"Dogs' Eyes"

I'm snowed in here in Jersey. Snow has a brightness and renewal. My dogs were running around in it this morning, happier than they have been these past few days. Their eyes and faces are wet with melting flakes.

It is hard to imagine each snowflake is an individual creation, each unlike the flake next to it. They look the same to the naked eye, but deep inspection through a microscope reveals the curves and bends that shape each one…sort of like the hearts and eyes of each of our dogs.

We may own several of the same breed. They may even look alike to passersby. But we could pick each one out in a crowd or a snowstorm.

All we have to do is look into their eyes.

"The Second Night of Grief"

It is early morning

Dark outside

Bailey is crying in his sleep

We got little rest last night

I am in a house full of mourners

Each wandering like a lost soul

Don't try to tell me animals

Feel no grief

They tell me without words

Each showing me his broken heart

And I must heal them all

Or they must all heal me...

My Bud had taken to sleeping with Apache Tears on her

blanket

My gentle soul, my nursemaid, my empath

Sharing a place of comfort and companionship

On a patch of warm friendship

Night before last, Bud was a restless soul

Last night, he curled up alone

On the only patch of solace he could find

I lay with him on their blanket for a while

On the empty patch

Comforting a lonely dog, a gentle soul

Telling him we had to let her go

Trying to convince us both

I had a long cry

Before climbing the stairs

To my own patch of solace

In my second night of restless grief...

A snowstorm is approaching

Soon it will blanket the ground

Perhaps offering a small patch of solace

To a home of grieving hearts

"I Am Old"

I am old

My eyes are quite clouded

My joints are now bent

My bladder is weak

My health has been spent

I am old

My bark is more still

My mind isn't strong

My teeth have all loosened

Nowhere I belong

I am old

I shake with a chill

My fur is all matted

I am over the hill

The dog you once boasted

Was show quality

Has now been reduced

To a heap of pity

But age does not take

A toll on my heart

Or the soul that would guard you

Till death I do part

Don't toss me away

Like a used, dirty rag

To carry another

Young, worthy of brag

My bones may be dwindling

But my spirit is brave

The heart of a puppy

Will lie in my grave

One day passing years

Will take toll on you

May the love in my spirit

Come tenfold to you

I still will be waiting

With paws open wide

To welcome the master

Who tossed me aside...

Care not I for years

Or the timekeeper's toll

For my love has not waivered

Although we are old...

Part One

The Beginnings

Beginning This Journey

I saw my first spirit when I was about eight years of age. I write more deeply about this experience in my first book. I did not share this experience with my parents or anyone else, choosing to keep this part of my existence private. I never understood the glimpses of past lives I would see, the science behind the telepathic abilities I possessed, or my ability to reach beyond the mind's fear of the veil that shields our eyes from the Spirit Realm.

Some see spirits. Some hear them. Others smell a spirit-carried fragrance. I have been fortunate enough to have sensed, at one time or another, spirits in all of these manners.

I have seen the wispy, grey haze of a face, hovering above my bed. I have heard the messages of loved ones who have crossed over into the Spirit Realm, allowing me to give comfort to the grief-stricken. I have heard the whistle of a little boy killed tragically in Gettysburg in the 19th century from a carriage accident outside the Farnsworth House. I have captured the tortured voice of an imprisoned soul at the Tower of London on my voice recorder. I have felt the touch of a spirit as it ran its fingers through my hair. I have smelled the fragrant smell of roses in the Farnsworth House in Gettysburg.

Once, while I was giving a lecture at a local library, I arrived early and was met by the overwhelming fragrance of roses. The librarian said that it had lingered all day, though not a rose was present. Spirits were present; they left a message to calm my nerves during one of my first public speaking events.

Spirits try to communicate with us in many different ways. Each of us is sensitive in his or her own way. One person may smell a fragrance, while another might feel the cold chill in the atmosphere. Some may continually reach for a phone that rings with no one on the other end.

Someone might be there—open your mind and ears to that call.

What Is A Ghost?

A ghost, or spirit presence, is energy. There are some who believe that the beginning of spirit energy formation manifests as orbs. I have captured some inexplicable orbs on film, even a few in motion. Some of the most intriguing have been photographed in my own home.

Spirit energy is all around us; you don't have to visit a haunted site to experience it. Some see spirit presence as wispy silhouettes; some see shadowy, black shapes out of the corners of their eyes; some see fully formed human bodies.

But a spirit, just like us, is energy. Some of that energy possesses intelligence. These are the ghost stories where a spirit communicates something to the one visited. Perhaps the message is where grandma's diamond earrings are hidden. Or perhaps where his or her own murdered body is buried. The spirit comes with a message, a purpose, and it needs to tell whoever will listen.

Some are not intelligent presences, but rather residual energy. By this, I mean a recording of the past. It is like watching a DVD—you can watch the action, but the spirits are not *there*. Only the recorded images remain. They cannot communicate with you, nor you with them.

Why do intelligent spirits remain on earth, not moving on to other dimensions? Perhaps, on my Gettysburg home fields, some Pennsylvania soldiers remain because they know the rolling hills. That is all they know; they fear the unknown.

Perhaps they are afraid that because they may have killed someone in battle, punishment awaits. Fear of this judgment can make a spirit remain.

Perhaps the moment of death was so quick and unexpected that they still don't believe they are not among the living. In Gettysburg, where one can always see people dressed in period costume and reenactors engaged in battle, I can understand how a spirit might be confused and think it is just a day or two after the first week in July, 1863.

Some, as I mentioned before, have a message to tell or a criminal to bring to justice.

Some may just love their bedroom so much that they won't leave. There may be new homeowners, there may be new furniture, but to them, it is still their bedroom.

Because we are all energy, as technology advances, I think it will be easier to communicate across the dimensions. It is like listening to a radio broadcast; some stations come in clearly, and some are filled with static. We just have to learn how to break through the static and stigma of communication with ghosts to achieve the connection.

Being Drawn to Haunted Places

I have often wondered if haunted places have an influence on events that seem to occur repeatedly. For example, sometimes you hear of a curve in the road that causes accidents over and over again. In my hometown, we have such a curve. Ironically, my daughter's first apartment overlooked this spot. Over and over, she would awaken to the sound of metal smashing and sirens rushing to the spot beneath her second story window.

Is it the energy of the curve or the energy of those who died there? (Perhaps the phrase *dead man's curve* has truth to it.) Or, is it simply coincidence or reckless driving?

I believe that troubled beings are drawn to places where troubled energy has existed and may still exist in the present day. I have seen it in Gettysburg. Troubled souls who have a difficult time finding a place in the ordinary often find their niche in the extraordinary.

Does the energy of a haunted place draw them to it, or does their troubled energy draw them to the place? I believe it is a little of both.

Grain House

I live in a historic farmhouse which dates back to colonial times. Like all old farmhouses, it has hiding holes and cracks large enough for a village of mice to fit through. And they do.

The Gettysburg winters can be fierce—howling winds and icy storms. Wouldn't you find a cozy farmhouse inviting?

After the Civil War, my farmhouse grew derelict and was left in abandonment. A nearby farmer took it over as his grain house. Hence, the name on my historical marker reads, "Grain House."

I've read stories of lentils surviving and sprouting seed in ancient pharaohs' tombs. No doubt, some grain granules remain. They might be a little stale, but beggar mice aren't choosers. Perhaps it is like the swallows in Capistrano. Mice families teach their young to go back to the granary.

I am sure they have carried the seeds in their tiny cheeks and hoarded towers of them in my walls and floors. Maybe not, but I have a vivid imagination. Perhaps they just love the quiet and warmth and shelter from the cold.

A lot of fellow Gettysburg residents have warned me of the mice. I am surrounded by fields. I was so naïve when I purchased my farm; I thought the mice stayed in the fields and didn't wander in. But things wander in at my farm. Living things and things in a state between life and death.

I have some ghosts, too. My farm was used during the Battle of Gettysburg as a Confederate Brigadier General's headquarters. He was wounded and carried back to one of my bedrooms to convalesce.

I think the mice and the spirits work together. I liken it to owning several dogs. One is always the fall guy when the others get into mischief. Mice and spirits like mischief. Sometimes, my husband and I don't know who (or what) is to blame. I swear there are times when they seem to partner up, just to mess with my head. The following chapters will reveal some of that mischief. You decide who is to blame.

Why Grain House Is So Haunted

You might say Grain House, like Gettysburg, is the perfect storm for paranormal activity.

A Confederate Brigadier General and his Cavalry found shelter here in the first July days of 1863. This wounded general's blood spilled on my floors, floors my feet still walk on today.

After the Civil War, Grain House took on another horrific chapter in American history. It became the headquarters of the local Ku Klux Klan. I feel as much sorrow from spirits tormented during this time as from the soldiers of the Battle—at times, even more so.

Next, my home became an abandoned granary. Hence, the mice treasures began accumulating. I have no doubt some grain remnants remain in the rafters. Then, Grain House became an antique store. Can you imagine all the spirits who wandered in and perhaps stayed as their possessions took residence at my farmhouse? Finally, Grain House reclaimed its purpose as a residential home.

When we closed on Grain House, a very interesting phenomenon occurred. I felt the presence of a young woman and her baby. A very sad presence. A friend of mine, without knowing my impressions, said she saw a black woman at the window in one of my photographs of the house.

It was then that we started getting cradles. My husband crafted a wooden cradle for a friend some thirty years earlier. Out of nowhere, this friend said he had mailed the cradle back in case we should have use for it. One night, coming home from work, my husband saw a tiny wooden cradle in the garbage. Now, it is usually a challenge for me to get my husband to stop for any roadside treasures my eyes seek out; his stopping on his own accord is quite a feat. I have several cradles at the farm now. I like to think a young, troubled mother and her baby sleep peacefully there at night.

From the time it was first deeded by William Penn to a Revolutionary War soldier, Grain House has had many a story to tell. Now, it is my turn to tell mine.

My First Visitor

The first time I walked into my farmhouse as owner, I was greeted by the perfect visitor.

I love birds. If you read my book of memoirs as an Animal Intuitive, you will learn about all the birds I have rescued.

Gettysburg is known for birdsong. The fields provide food and sanctuary for many songbirds, and my farm is a gathering place of nests among the bushes and trees. A dove nest is nestled right above my front door; each year, it is recycled by another family with baby hatchlings.

On my return from the real estate closing on the farm, I climbed the stairs to my bedroom and saw a little bluebird try to burst into my window. He wasn't hurt; he was just a little too enthusiastic about bringing me a welcome home greeting from the animal kingdom.

Since then, many of his friends have come to greet me. My mice lead the welcome wagon committee. They have recruited woodchucks, moles, hawks, herons, deer, skunks, and many others to join the party at my farmhouse.

I am glad my little bluebird of happiness sought out me and my bedroom window that afternoon.

The Perfect Storm

J ust as Gettysburg is often referred to as "the perfect paranormal storm," Grain House is my perfect storm of happiness. I love history, wormholes in time, spirit energy, and things that are old. (This last one pertains to furry companions, as well.)

Walk through my farmhouse door and the centuries are peeled away. Spirits feel at home here because not much has changed. Step into my garden and energy-charged quartz crystals lay at your feet. Combine this with the trauma and death of three horrific July days, and you have the perfect paranormal storm.

Our first night at the farmhouse offered no ghostly encounters. Only one tiny, frightened mouse, trapped in the pantry, greeted us. He escaped.

My second night at the farmhouse was my "perfect, paranormal storm." My husband and I were going out there to check on things and also to assist my father-in-law who was awaiting cancer surgery in the coming week. When we were one hour outside of Gettysburg, my husband received a cell phone call from his dad. The medical center had notified him of a change in the surgery schedule; they could fit him in early the next morning. I knew then that I was going to face what I told my husband I did not want to experience—a night alone at the farm.

My father-in-law's admittance time was 5:30 a.m. at the medical center. Gettysburg was about an hour away from my father-in-law's house at that time. At first, my husband agreed that 4:30 a.m. would leave him sufficient travel time. However, as the night progressed, I could sense my husband becoming antsy. We both got little rest in our "comfy" sleeping bags of nails on the hardwood floor.

Then, 3:30 a.m. became the better option. My perfect storm was intensifying. Midnight came and went. Around 1 a.m., my husband decided he would be leaving at two. He would not wake his dad, but he would wait outside his home until it was time to pick him up for surgery. He just couldn't rest at the farmhouse. I knew my hope of rest that night was over, as well.

I don't know what caused me the most distress that evening: the thought of being alone for such a long stretch of night, ghosts, that pantry mouse on the loose, or the potential serial killer roaming the Gettysburg fields that night.

I was half angry and half terrified as my husband came into the nearly pitch black darkness and said he was leaving. I laid there in my hard-as-nails sleeping bag, quietly crying, contemplating what weapons I could muster in case some murderer knocked on the farmhouse door that night. I had a plastic butter knife—that was about it—and my cell phone. However, I envisioned that by the time I got up and reached for either, I would probably be dead, zipped up in my sleeping bag, and my killer would be well over the Mason Dixon Line.

As I lay there, I heard my husband still in the kitchen. I could hear the sound of the teapot on the stove. I could hear the sound of metal spoons tinkling inside cups as tea or coffee was stirred. (Now, I look back and know how impossible this was; we only had plastic spoons and cups, and we hadn't any sugar to stir even if desired.) I could hear the sound of the plastic garbage bag rustling and the sound of my husband puttering around the kitchen. I was so relieved that he decided to stay longer.

This went on for about 30-45 minutes from my best estimation of time. Finally, I heard him heavily sigh as he sat down in the wooden chair we had brought on an earlier trip. Furniture and supplies were still scarce at the farm.

Feeling bad that he had so much to worry about besides a pathetic wife afraid to be alone in the dark, I got up to tell him that he had better get going or he was going to fall asleep in that chair and be late. I went into the kitchen and found it dark and empty. The chair was back in the other room by my sleeping bag.

I can only tell you that this wasn't frightening. An overall sense of calmness filled me. I felt as if some presence had sensed my distress and sought to give me some moments of comfort in the night. I thanked whoever this was and went back to my sleeping bag.

I shut my eyes momentarily and, for whatever reason, reopened them. In the dimness of the night light-lit room, I saw what appeared to be a dark pom-pom on the floor about two feet from my head. The pom-pom moved! Realizing it was my mouse friend from the pantry, I discovered just how fast these aching bones could jump in the night. No one heard my scream that night, except a mouse—and maybe a ghost or two. As for my cheese-seeking friend, he made a quick dash for the rolling hills of Gettysburg via the corner hole in my floorboard.

No further rest for these weary bones came that night. I spent the last remaining hours of darkness in that wooden chair. My husband and father-in-law had a few good laughs at my expense on the way to Hershey Medical Center that morning. I have not slept on that floor since.

I asked my spirit friends if they could please do something about that mouse for me. They did something all right. They have joined forces in shenanigans to entertain my Gettysburg visits.

Now, I can rationalize the rustling of the plastic garbage bag that night; maybe tiny mouse paws were foraging for crumbs. But I don't know many mice that prepare a cup of tea or bring their own metal spoons to stir in the cups as they drink.

So, what explains the noises I heard? It is a creaky, old house, but what I heard cannot be explained by creaks and settling. I know I was not dreaming.

Did someone take pity on a frightened housemate and offer solace? I like to believe so. The previous farmhouse owners recounted stories to us of smelling bacon frying and breakfast cooking in the kitchen on several occasions. Maybe my ghosts like to make midnight snacks as well as morning tea. That's okay, as long as they clean up when they are done.

And so my quest to find out continues. Whether it was mice or ghosts, there will be farmhouse stories to tell.

One Man's Poison is Another Mouse's Candy Cane

My search began for the most effective, natural mouse repellent out there.

Not much luck with this.

My husband came home with those electronic plug-in mouse frequency repellents. Internet reviews are solidly in favor of their ineffectiveness. I made him return them to the store. Besides, they frighten me a little. I work as an Intuitive; I *hear* other frequencies. What if he plugged those in and I ran screaming from the house?

We decided next on peppermint oil. It is safe, non-toxic, and people shared some hopeful comments online about its effectiveness.

Always remember—when directions tell you to put just a teensy amount in a spray bottle filled with water, follow them. I almost asphyxiated myself with peppermint oil one afternoon and ended up running—though not screaming—out of the house.

My mice? Well, I think they made candy canes. It was Christmastime; the house felt refreshing and *Christmasy.*

Did peppermint oil work? No. Did it make my guests happy? I think so. Now they slept with peppermint drops, not sugar plums, dancing through their heads.

Besides, peppermint works as a good digestive aid. It probably helped their tiny stomachs digest all the other things they ate at my farm. More of that later...

We still use the peppermint oil. Recently, my husband almost asphyxiated himself. Humans never learn. One man's poison is another mouse's candy cane.

City Girl/Country Mice

L iving with mice and ghosts is a unique experience. Both can bring smiles and screams. You learn very quickly to carefully open closets and pantry drawers because you never know what is waiting to say hello.

Mice will find any crumb. Even if you are meticulous about cleaning, they will find other things. I have had expensive soaps chewed by hungry little teeth, and I have lost many a perfumed candle to a hungry mouse. I never knew they consumed such things, but the fat in both sustains them when no other nourishment is available.

Sometimes, they get to my things before I even get to enjoy them. Like the new, plush bathroom rug I purchased— its soft loops provided cozy nests for baby mice. Like my brand-new pair of gardening gloves—I opened the drawer and saw a cozy mouse nest skillfully constructed inside of them.

I think my mice have set up a little country store in the fields around my farm. It is a wonderful place, filled with finely-milled soaps and perfumed candles, amber-colored jars brimming with buttons, coquettish ribbons for fine mice hair, and snippets of yarn and lace. Peppermint oil diffusers fill the air with the scent of Christmas and candy canes. They hold their own ghost tours on my farm to visit the memorials to their dead within the walls. Yes, they have their own miniature village, full of life and laughter and love.

Holiday weekends are busy at the mice shoppe. One Valentine's Day, my expensive, rose-shaped floating candles were chewed. It seems a Valentine's feast was a special event held at my farm. I envision it clearly—chivalrous gentlemen mice (with their whiskers neatly groomed) and fair maiden coquettes (scented with florals and mints) gaze longingly into each other's eyes. Even my ghosts must smile at this display of love.

Part Two

Moves with Intention

The Whispers of Ghosts

When people hear the word ghost, little hairs stand up on the backs of their necks and all sorts of malevolent thoughts come to mind. Sounds of rattling chains and gruesome moans are conjured. Except for some few-and-far-between haunting instances, thankfully, this isn't so. The presence of spirits does not mean blood-drenched walls and pots flying across the room. It can, but thankfully, that is not the norm.

Usually, the presence of spirits comes in the form of little *wisps on the wind* that say *hello, I am here.*

My farmhouse is quite old. It has seen many births and deaths. It has seen war. It has sheltered a Confederate General and soldiers and offered safety for the bloody and wounded. So, yes, there are *wisps on the wind*. Not mean spirited; in fact, often just the opposite.

Old home or new, most have these *visits*; the land itself holds energy, energy of those who walked and loved and died there. Gettysburg happens to be filled with an unusually high number of spirit residents because of the trauma that took place on sweltering, summer days in 1863.

I like walking among the ghosts...after all, they walked here first. We co-exist in the world of energy, in a farmhouse that has seen life and death and what remains.

Often, it is subtle messages—objects moved around, appliances plugged in and unplugged. Sometimes, on very special visits, little gifts are left behind.

We have a small walk-in crawl space. Not always, but often, little messages are left when we enter. Last time, paint cans were moved into a new location. The crawl space is locked; unless one of our farm mice dons a cape, it is doubtful this feat could have been accomplished by rodent hands. (Maybe there is some genetically-modified corn growing somewhere in nearby fields, giving super strength to rodent paws. I doubt it. I think this is one of those ghost/mice partnerships I wrote of earlier.) Bags of salt for our water softener always move—to the same spot each time. It seems our ghosts have a sense of humor. Without a whisper of wind, how do these objects find their way back to the same moved locations each time we visit?

These aren't frightful messages, just little *hellos* to make a presence known and probably bring smiles to a ghostly face in the ether. These acts of mischief must brighten the lonely existences of souls tied to certain places, souls who long for human companionship, for human touch.

These spirits bring comfort, as well. In times of intense emotions, they seem to know a little wisp of comfort would be welcomed. They touch us the only way they can...with whispers on the wind.

And sometimes, these whispers are spoken into the ears of little mice. I am certain of it.

* Not only soldiers wander the Gettysburg fields of my farmhouse. Animals have come to visit and leave messages, as well.

I believe that the spirits of animals can return, just like the spirits of the humans who cared for them. I have been privileged to be a part of many wondrous experiences with animal spirits; the bonds formed between man and animals are not broken by death.

My front entrance has a double door. The outer one opens to the outside; you must open this one to access a second inner door. This entrance is not used by me, my pets, or anyone else visiting with pets. Yet, one day, my husband and I noticed an unmistakably large paw print on that inner door—too big for a small animal, too high up on the door for a little one.

How it got there is a mystery. No animal could gain access to that door from the outside, and no animal of mine had touched that door.

Perhaps a spirit animal just wanted to leave a little hello for me.

You Never Have a Camera Ready

Ghosts don't like to perform on cue. They come when you aren't looking, when your mind is busy on some task, when you are rushing around in your daily routine, not when you have a video camera in hand.

My farm ghosts are like that. Usually, they choose to perform their stunts and pranks at times when we are all alone so there are no corroborating witnesses.

For instance, my husband was wheeling a wheelbarrow full of branches past the side door of our barn. The barn door was closed. The light switch for the outside door is inside the barn. Yet, as my husband passed directly by it, the light flashed on and off twice. He opened the barn door; the switch was off.

He swears it happened. I believe him, though I teased him about it being the sun on the bulbs. This is what the ghosts want. They smile as one confounded witness tries to persuade another of the incident.

That same afternoon, I had a ghostly incident of my own. Of course, no witnesses. I had to go inside the house to get a broom from the living room closet. It is a sizable room, documented as being the location where the inhabitants of my farmhouse hid their flour and possessions before the

Confederates raided them in 1863. A large piece of furniture was pushed in front of the door to conceal their treasures.

I got the broom, though I noticed that when I opened the closet door, the light cord was swaying back and forth. I thought, "Oh well, maybe just a breeze," even though no windows were open. I got the broom out and latched the door. I distinctly remember latching it.

I went outside, resumed my garden chores, and then came in after a while. The closet door was wide open. This particular door swings back to close; there is no way it would ever swing open—it is a physical impossibility. I asked my husband if he had come in for anything. His answer was no. So, how did the door open?

Like I said, no witnesses. They like to play games with the farmhouse and our minds. They have had such tormented lives and deaths...how can I begrudge them this innocent mischief?

Blood-Stained Quilt

I bought a beautiful embroidered white quilt for my farmhouse bed. During one visit, I walked into the bedroom and saw a stain across the top. It looked like old, dried blood. The stain went through the quilt onto my sheets in the same shape and location.

In 1863, one of my farmhouse beds was the resting place of a bloody, wounded Confederate General.

I still haven't washed that quilt, and I don't intend to. Sometimes, I think about having that stain analyzed. But then again, some things are best left open to wonderment.

Blood-Splattered Floor

There was blood shed within the walls of my farmhouse in 1863. A Confederate Brigadier General was wounded and carried up the staircase into one of my bedrooms.

There is still blood today, and not just on my quilts and sheets. I have found splatters of blood on my bedroom floor. Blood has been left before, but it has been dried blood, rust-colored spots that defy explanation—at least explanation from this realm.

photo © Shirl Knobloch 2013

Splattered Blood left for me on my farmhouse floor
April 13th, 2013

Does it bother me? No. The energies are benevolent. But they communicate what they know, and unfortunately, they are still living in the blood and battle of another century.

You learn to accept these things. Do I run screaming from the room? No. When tired enough, you come home to a blood-stained quilt and you sleep under it. This might sound bizarre or frightening, but it is just day-to-day living in this strangely haunted town.

You should visit here at least once...maybe you will leave with a mind forever changed and accepting of the unseen world.

General Lee's A-Coming

I must be the only person in America with a refrigerator chalkboard that reads: *"Went to get a cannon 'cause General Lee's a-coming."*

That is my son's sense of humor, but the words are true. He and my husband really did set off on a road trip, U-haul in tow, to get a cannon.

Can you imagine being stopped on the interstate with a cannon??? Luckily, they made the road trip with no incident. The cannon now sits on my farm property, aimed in the correct position...'*cause you never know when General Lee's a-coming.*

As an interesting footnote, the day the blood splatters appeared on my bedroom floor was the same day the cannon was placed into position on my property. The Brigadier General who made my farmhouse his headquarters was wounded in the head by cannon shrapnel and lay bleeding in one of the bedrooms at my farmhouse.

Perhaps my Confederate ghost wasn't too happy about that cannon on my land.

The Winds of Gettysburg

I have come to notice that places extremely haunted or powerfully supernatural carry forceful winds. The winds in Gettysburg can be fierce; you can hear them howling. The wind seems to come from the mountains onto the rolling hills and strengthens the energy of whatever is tormented on this land.

Some light workers feel the winds are Angel wings fluttering over the ground. Stonehenge felt like that. I visited on a cold, wintry day; my hood barely shielded me from the intense winds—Angel wings or Druid wings at work perhaps.

I remember the first years after 9/11, watching the memorials on TV. The anniversary days were always quite windy. Passing years have subsided them. Perhaps the grief and hauntings have subsided so the wings of Angels need not flutter so intensely.

I stood very close to the Towers as they fell. I was directly across the water, near the Statue of Liberty, at Liberty State Park. I think light workers are drawn to areas of intense energy. Winds, stormy seas, eclipses, and disturbances in the whole energetic grid affect those of us known as sensitives. We are extremely empathic to these shifts. And perhaps they affect the energy of spirits, as well.

My Farmhouse Table

I used to keep a large white candle on my kitchen table. It was tied with a beautiful satin ribbon. Each time I came home, the bow would be untied and lay neatly alongside the candle. Whether mice or ghosts, something was having fun through this mischievous torment.

I have since moved the candle. The bow has not been disturbed in its new place, but the candle has been chewed.

Perhaps it's mice retaliation.

Perfect Time

I have an angel clock in my kitchen that runs on a battery. As time progressed, the clock started losing perfect time. We would change the battery, and the clock would still keep imperfect time.

One day, my husband just left the dead battery in, and we went back to our suburban home. When we returned the next time to the farmhouse, our kitchen clock was running. Okay, you say, the battery wasn't dead; it merely started working again. But the time on the clock was PERFECT, down to the minute. Figure this one out—we can't. Except for the likely explanation of ghosts, there really isn't a feasible reason for this clock starting at precisely the exact moment in time it should have.

Batteries often die in Gettysburg. New batteries or newly-charged batteries, it doesn't matter. The spirits need the energy; we Gettysburg residents have learned to share.

"The Hands of Time"

I am slow moving

This morning

I lost an hour

Mortals are such fools

Lose an hour

Gain an hour

As if we are

Masters of Time

Time waits

    or

Speeds for no one

She decides the hour

Our Hands will

    Move Ahead

    or

    Set back

    To eternal rest.

Tidy Ghosts

Early one Sunday morning, I looked out of my farmhouse window onto my deck and had a morning surprise waiting for me...my first "hello whisper" of the day. I have several heavy woven mats on my deck. Sometimes, during very blustery storms, the mats may shift—not so out of the ordinary.

On this particular morning, however, one of my "guests" found an unusual way to say good morning to me. The deck has levels separated by a step, and the deck rails have very tiny slats between the boards. Picture in your mind the following scenario as it greeted my eyes in the morning sun: one of my mats was carefully pulled through one of these tiny slats and hung in the middle of the rails.

This may not sound so fascinating, but I can tell you that even if a tornado force wind (which I hadn't felt the night prior) blew our way, the chance of this mat lifting and neatly landing through one of these tiny slats—hanging as if someone intentionally inserted it there—is monumentally small.

This is one of those *moves with intention* one gets used to upon living in Gettysburg. Strange little incidents, so small one brushes them off with a fleeting grin. I think the ghosts grin, too; they take such delight in messing with our minds, especially before morning coffee clears out the cobwebs in our brains.

These little "hellos" are just ways to make our day more eventful. When you wake up in a haunted Civil War farmhouse, you never know who might be stopping by to say "good morning."

I Think My Mice Are Druids

I receive little presents from my ghosts and my mice. For some reason, there is a spot in my farmhouse comparable to the space underneath a Christmas tree. In this same place, several gifts have been left for me.

The place I speak of is on my kitchen floor, right in front of my large country sink. I know water draws spirits; the most haunted locations in the world are beside bodies of water. I guess in the middle of the rolling hills in Gettysburg, my sink stands in as the local watering hole, offering a vortex of spiritual energy.

I think my farmhouse mice are Druids. I picture them in long, brown, hooded robes, carrying oak staffs as they cross the darkened fields at night.

Observing the Solstice at Gettysburg.

One night, they left me a rather unusual gift—I found a tiny mouse skull in front of my sink. Maybe a Druid sacrifice?

 I took it as an honored show of respect. Their offering to me I still have. Then I got to thinking. My farm sits on such hallowed ground, where the remains of untold numbers of fallen victims still lie without honor in the ground. Maybe the mice have hallowed ground, as well, a place to honor their fallen. Why shouldn't they? I hold this tiny skull with honor and respect for one who died on hallowed ground.

Perhaps, like elephants, the tiniest of creatures mourn for their dead. Maybe in my walls, interspersed between the mounds of grain, lay towers of rodent cairns and skeletons to mark their deaths with honor.

Forget-Me-Nots

My most poignant gift was an antique ring enameled with pretty blue flowers that look like forget-me-nots. What a touching gift from sentimental mice or thoughtful ghosts or both! I promise to forget them not.

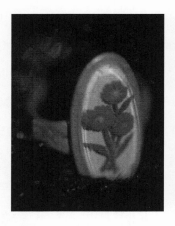 

Another time, an antique button lay in front of my sink. I knew it was recently "put" there because I had just polished the entire kitchen floor. Looking through internet photos of Civil War era buttons, I could see it bore a striking resemblance. Either the *Tailor of Gloucester* mice had emigrated from England and were sewing up jackets in my walls, or my Gettysburg mice had decided to leave me a little memento.

Sometimes, just interesting little things are left for me. Once, an old medicine tablet was left in front of my sink. Maybe my mice thought I had a headache. It was considerate of them to offer help, even more so since they are often the source of my Gettysburg headaches.

Even more unusual than the presents is the fact that they are always left in the same spot. Whenever we come home to the farmhouse, we know just where to find them. Like I said earlier, it is like searching under the Christmas tree on Christmas morning.

I like receiving these little gifts. They always appear when least expected, just as any good surprise should.

Mice Humor

I collect mice figurines; I have done so for many years, long before the real ones came into my life.

My Gettysburg mice have an ironic sense of humor. I will come home and find nothing disturbed in the house except that all of my mice figurines will be knocked over. Not broken, just knocked to the ground. There they lay, humiliated, their fake mouse spirits broken. Maybe my mice are telling me they can't be fooled by fake imitations.

I have two stuffed Boyds Bear mice sitting on top of the baker's rack by my back door. Twice, I have come home to find them face down, disgraced, at their sentry post of guarding the farm against rodent intruders. I can almost hear little mouse giggles and tiny voices saying "ha ha."

Their ghostly counterparts have fun with statues, too. I have angel statues on my windowsills, and sometimes, I find them knocked over. Never broken, which is amazing, just knocked gently over or laid down by unseen hands. Sometimes, they aren't knocked over but "rearranged." Angel faces that watched over my room will now be watching over each other, face-to-face on the windowsill. Once, every window in the room had them turned to this position.

Yes, ghosts and mice have a unique sense of humor; their hellos are sent with smiles.

I wish they would learn to do some dusting and vacuuming, too, along with all that redecorating.

Tricksters

My daughter's first time alone in the farmhouse was around noontime. I had gone out to the grocery store to get some lunch supplies. She was left to wander around and explore the place.

When I got home, she said, "You missed a couple." Dumbfounded, I asked what she meant. She said, "You missed a couple. I didn't know you unplugged all the plugs when you left the farmhouse. There are two in the front room you missed."

I told her that I didn't unplug all of the plugs. She proceeded to go around to show me all the unplugged lights. Well, you can guess what she saw. Every plug was plugged in.

I doubt she took a noontime nap and the incident was but a dream. I tend to believe that the spirits were just having some afternoon fun with a new captive audience, that's all.

I would wager a pretty safe bet that when she now visits my farmhouse, her eyes first drift toward those wall sockets still.

Telling the difference between wandering, furry feet and ghostly pranks is easy. Scurrying little paws can unintentionally break delicate objects. However, seeing a fragile object "fall" from a windowsill to the hardwood floor without so much as a nick on it is too amazing to not raise an eyebrow or two. Then again, when you come home to a shelf full of knickknacks and only the mice statues are touched, it makes you wonder who's kidding you....the mice or the spirits.

Ghosts Have Ears

Ever hear the phrase "the walls have ears"? Well, I can surely tell you ghosts have ears, too. They usually leave me answers, letting me know they are well aware of the goings on at the farmhouse.

While washing dishes at my sink one afternoon, my mind started thinking how quiet things had been lately around the farm. I had received no usual hellos from the spirit plane. Within seconds, a nice soup bowl crashed down to the floor with such noise and impact that I screamed. Sometimes, their idea of fun isn't so amusing to me. I am sure that certain little spirit mouths turn upwards in wispy smiles of delight when they get my mortal dander up.

On another afternoon, my husband and I were out weeding the garden. We were pressed for time, having a long drive back to our home in the suburbs. I came inside, tossed off my gloves, and put them on a chair in the kitchen.

My husband came in soon afterwards and asked where I placed my gloves. I answered, "Why, are you packing them up to bring home with us?" I pointed to the chair. He picked them up and placed them with his own gardening gloves in the bag on the kitchen table.

We packed up more stuff to take back. He once again opened the kitchen bag, but in it, he found only three gloves— his pair and one of mine.

Now, I know I took both gloves off of my hands. I saw him pick them up, and I watched him place them inside the little bag on the table.

We searched around. Moments such as these when we are pressed for time can make ghost pranks a little exasperating.

We finally found the glove. It was neatly packed in a bag on the dining room table, a bag of snacks my husband takes with him to munch on while driving home. This bag had not been touched since he brought it back from the nearby grocery store.

I guess my ghosts do listen. They heard me ask if he was taking my gloves home. They just thought it comical to pack them where *they* wished.

Sometimes You Have to Accept the Unexplained

One afternoon, while getting ready to pack our vehicle for the ride back to New Jersey, my husband had an unexplainable surprise awaiting. I was close by, observing, but not an actual witness to this event. I had a couple of bizarre occurrences of my own to process from the previous day.

I watched him, with a look of bewilderment on his face, walking to and fro from the front of the vehicle to the front seat. This kept up for a few moments. I thought to myself that something must be wrong mechanically with the car and the heavy bags I just carried out would now have to be carried back in.

I approached him and asked what was going on. He said that his fog lights were on. Now, I have never known my husband to leave his vehicle lights on. My first thought was, "Great! Dead battery time." He repeated, "You don't understand, my fog lights CANNOT be on!" The headlight switch must be turned on before he can activate the fog light switch. He checked the headlight switch about three times—it was OFF.

He once again walked to the front of the vehicle. The lights were off now.

Being the "sharp" investigator that I am, I asked him if maybe the sun was shining and he just imagined the lights on. He replied, "This was not sun. The lights were on. Here, feel them—they are still hot."

So, in a vehicle where one switch has to be turned on in order to turn on a second switch to activate the fog lights— and both switches are OFF—how are the lights on, and why is the battery not drained after a night, a morning, and an early afternoon of usage?

I was outside for much of that morning, tending to my own paranormal surprises. I can tell you I never saw lights on. My husband is not one to imagine things. He has had a lot to contend with just being married to me and accepting weird stuff as part of the package. The light switches worked fine, and the battery was fine, so what energized those fog lights? Guess you know my thoughts.

Coincidentally (or not), this happened after a long day of investigation (and a séance) at the Farnsworth Inn. Sometimes, spirits follow you home. Perhaps one thought he would illuminate our eyes to the Spirit World that afternoon.

Don't Make a Ghost Angry

Remember Bill Bixby as the Hulk saying, "Don't make me angry. You don't want to make me angry"? Well, that saying holds true for ghosts, too.

I never use Ouija boards; my own energy is strong enough. I never liked the thought of using something else to draw in spirit presence. I thought, however, that a spirit board would make a nice complement to my paranormal ghost workshop and tour presentations.

I searched for and purchased a beautiful one, and I brought it with me to Gettysburg. I had only to lay my hand on the planchette before feeling extraordinary energy come through it. I knew instantly this was not something I should ever use myself. Gettysburg guests and paranormal attendees would be one thing—me, quite another.

The moment I brought that board into the house, there was a palpable change in the energy. Weird things started happening to me, physical things. My husband was outside doing yard work. I was in the kitchen at my sink. It always seems to be at my sink. Suddenly, a cabinet door swung open with terrific force and bashed into my leg. I had an instantaneous black and blue mark. I showed my husband; he said I bumped into it. I didn't bump into it. That same day, a latch on my kitchen door cut my arm. I had passed that latch countless times before with no problem. There was a problem this day.

I packed the board up and took it home. The peaceful energy returned. There was something about the presence of that spirit board that so angered my ghost residents. Perhaps they were afraid some evil companion would try to co-exist in their peaceful patch of farmland if I called him in.

The board remains packed away, along with some cleansing quartz crystals. It is quite beautiful, but it carries things that aren't so beautiful, as well.

I have always believed that it is the intention which affects the spiritual energy, not the implements used. Implements are neither good nor evil; the user's intent determines the tone of the experience. So, equating spirit boards or pendulums or tarot cards with evil is a myth erroneously believed by many.

I still believe this. But one of my Gettysburg ghosts definitely did not like that spirit board in my home. I chose to honor his wishes and restore the peace.

Not All Pranksters Are Ghosts

One Halloween evening, my husband and I drove out at midnight to Sach's Bridge. I wouldn't recommend that anyone venture out there alone; it is pitch black and quite deserted. On the bridge, you cannot even see your hand in front of you. We had our infrared cameras; they provided a beam of light directly in view ahead of us—faint, but helpful.

On the bridge, I started taking photographs. In my camera lens appeared the body of a soldier, fully dressed, head down, and avoiding all eye contact with me. I think what baffled him most was the rise he didn't get out of me. He expected me to scream, to run, to cry, anything to make his Halloween momentous. I just stood there taking pictures. It is

eerie, though; not once did his face appear in any of them. Always his kepi was shadowing his eyes, always looking down. I am almost certain this was a mortal in a reenactor's costume, having fun on a ghostly night in Gettysburg. My husband and I didn't hang around to see him leave—I sometimes wish we had. Reenactors pulling pranks such as these are considered disdainful in Gettysburg, but I am sure it happens from time to time.

I often wonder if it's the troubled history of a place that heightens the paranormal activity, or if it's the pull of those with troubled energy themselves, seeking out such places in order to feel a sense of belonging. Gettysburg pulls those who love its history and those who seek a common bond with its sadness.

If you venture into the Grove Woods at night to take pictures, you might come home with a one-legged apparition in your camera. No, this isn't a ghost capture. Someone tossed a one-legged statue out in the woods. At night, especially with a night vision camera, he looks quite eerie. I haven't seen him in years; I wonder if he is still there. I also wonder how many have thought that they caught a one-legged ghost on film.

Some pranks are just plain cruel. Any defacing of our nation's monuments is something I find especially

heartless. It happens every now and then. Thankfully, the number of those who respect and revere greatly outweighs the number of those who have no conscience in destruction.

Part Three

Hauntings on Hallowed Grounds

Mark Nesbitt's Ghosts of Gettysburg Building

I work as an Intuitive. Sometimes, empathic emotions are thrust upon me as I enter a particular site or building. One such site is the well-known Ghosts of Gettysburg building, owned by Mark Nesbitt.

I once went on a regular ghost tour there. I was feeling fine when I entered, but as I walked inside, a slight lower back pain nudged at me. As the evening progressed, I could barely conceal the extraordinary pain I was experiencing. We were led upstairs for an entertaining ghost talk; all I could do was lean against a wall and hope I didn't collapse in agony.

I don't let on who I am or what I do during ghost tours or walks unless I am the one holding them. I didn't want to have to explain why I needed to rush out. Thankfully, I just about made it down the stairs and out the front door. As soon as I reached the pavement, my pain was completely gone. We proceeded to go out to dinner right afterward.

The Ghosts of Gettysburg building has been the site of a soldier's apparition. He is thought to be wounded. I can tell you that his wounds were in the lower back region. His pain was excruciating; he chose to share it with me that evening.

The Tillie Pierce House

One place I will never spend the night at again is the Tillie Pierce House. From the moment we checked in, strange things happened. Doors to haunted rooms next to ours suddenly opened, beckoning our entrance. We didn't go. Lights turned on when the wall switch was off. The water heating system broke down, and we had only ice cold water for a couple of days.

The first night I slept in the Salome Myers room, a very negative energy tried to test my will. I had just come back from an investigation at the Grove. The Grove is said to harbor the evil spirit of an innocent looking girl—innocent until you get close enough to see her glowing, demonic eyes. Many have run away in fear. I do not know for sure whether it was this spirit who chose to hitch a ride with me back to the Pierce House or if what I experienced was a resident energy of the Inn. All I can do is relay the circumstances that ensued. However, there are two reasons I suspect that it may have been the Grove spirit, or Elizabeth with the glowing eyes.

My husband was sound asleep. The room was ice cold. It was summer, but I had on a hooded sweatshirt because I was freezing in this room. As with many paranormal encounters, certain physical symptoms ensued. My heart was pounding rapidly, a sign of supernatural energy.

I developed a sharp, stabbing pain in back of my eyes. I was nauseous and sweating, even though I was frozen with cold. I always wear an obsidian gemstone around my neck when investigating the supernatural. Thankfully, I had not taken it off that evening before going to bed. I sat up in bed and looked at the mirror directly across from me. My eyes took on a shape-shifting look, changing, becoming someone else's, not mine. Perhaps they were the eyes of Elizabeth; I do not know.

Suddenly, my obsidian pendant's cord grew tighter and tighter around my neck. I was desperately trying to loosen it without much success. At this point, my husband awakened and asked what was wrong. I angrily told him to leave me alone. Whatever this energy was, it was taking hold of me, and I was struggling to remain the victor. I knew the battle was mine alone; he couldn't help me, and something made me answer in such a negative way that he just left me to my own devices. My angry words almost bit my inquisitive husband's head off that night. I was absorbed in a tidal wave of anger and evil energy; whoever this spirit was, it was a tortured soul.

I think that my obsidian absorbed much of the negative energy that night. Perhaps it broke the strength of something trying to cause me pain or at least trying to challenge my own psychic defenses. In the morning, I tried to untie the cord, which I always tie in a simple knot. The knot had been tied and tied again; it took some time to unloosen it. The cord was still soaking wet, drenched in my sweat.

Perhaps trying to inflict pain on me by tightening the cord backfired, and the obsidian's protective nature ensured that no harm was done. Whichever it was, I would not spend another night in that Inn if you paid me.

The Grove continues to be the place where I feel the most uneasy in Gettysburg. It is pleasant by day but ominous by night. If you venture into the woods and see a little girl, run before you look into her eyes.

* Mirrors are portals to the spirit realm. I was raised to believe in the metaphysical properties of mirrors. Ancient people have always connected the *mirror image* with magick, fearing that capturing one's reflection captured one's essence or soul. I don't fear being in a darkened room, but I do not like being in the presence of mirrors. There is a mirror in the morgue at Farnsworth House that I would not like to peer into longer than a second or two.

There were two large mirrors in my office. One was the point of a vortex or doorway to another dimension or realm. Even animals coming in for Reiki sessions were affected by this corner of the room. My office was haunted; it was a very old doctor's office refurbished into a modern office complex. I think some patients stayed. I will never forget the icy blast of air that once hit me as I entered one evening; it was unlike any cold I had ever felt before. There were good and bad energies at that place. Thankfully, I think Reiki and the animals tipped the balance and made the light sway the scales in favor of benevolent visits.

Be very mindful of mirrors if you investigate or if you cleanse your home with smudging, sage, and crystals. Don't neglect to cleanse each mirror in your home.

Séance at the Farnsworth House

I was asked to lead a ghost investigation at one of Gettysburg's most noted hauntings, Farnsworth House. It was a wonderful experience with a great bunch of people, all of whom were eager and open to the idea of spirit communication.

We had many fascinating experiences. I began the evening with a séance. We had some cold breezes and some touches to participants, along with a persistent door rattle that beckoned us to start roaming the bedrooms. We also had some memorable communication from personal family members during the séance.

When you call in ghosts, you never know who may choose to say hello. A woman's audible moan was heard by me and other group members, as well as, we believe, Jeremy whistling back to a young boy in our group who had whistled out to him. (Jeremy is a small child who was killed outside the Farnsworth House by a carriage while playing tag.) Several group members were audibly aware of a whistling in the room, and no one in the group was the type to play tricks. I believe the moaning came from Mary, a midwife who answered as I talked to her about the stillborn child delivered by her at Farnsworth.

I captured a couple of moving orbs on video which were also visible to others in the group. One of these orbs appeared just as I was talking to the group about what an orb is thought to be. Coincidence? You decide.

I led many question sessions, asking for yes or no responses by thumps. We did get some replies. There is much outside noise from Baltimore Street, but the tour members felt thumps directly under their bodies or heard them quite vividly from different spots in the rooms.

At one point, the dress in the Sarah Black room moved. There was a person sitting in close proximity to it, so I have to factor in human participation (albeit unknowingly) in this event. There was no breeze, no open window, and we had turned off the air conditioning in the rooms, but still the group consistently felt cold and freezing breezes across their bodies.

After the evening's end, more weird things continued; sensations of beings in the room, audible singing, and blankets pulling down by themselves were experienced in the Sarah Black room, as well as in other bedrooms at the Farnsworth (by tour members who slept overnight there).

Stranger still, upon arriving home, several members of the group experienced strange bruising on various parts of their bodies. As I told them during the investigation, calling in these spirits can result in things happening later on, after an investigation has ended.

All in all, everyone had a great time. The Farnsworth House was great, the company was great, and I hope my investigational skills satisfied everyone present.

Wandering Spirits

I do believe that spirits wander around Gettysburg. Spirits drift for many reasons. Many weren't ready to die. Some were afraid of what was waiting on the other side—perhaps judgment and punishment. They had unfinished business here on earth, perhaps young wives and babies at home. They died so quickly that still, after centuries, some don't realize they are gone from physical energy.

Gettysburg is the perfect storm for wandering souls, young boys taken from life too soon in horrific manners—limbs blown apart, sometimes lying in pain on the battlefield in a slow, agonizing death. These deaths were not peaceful. A death not at peace may leave a spirit in a state of unrest.

I have yet to see a wandering spirit in Gettysburg, but I have come face-to-face with one in my hometown of New Jersey. I was closing up my Reiki office for the night. It was late, and I had just finished a class. The rest of my office building was empty.

I knew my office building had several spirits, most of them benevolent. One was a little boy. My office building was old; it had been a physician's office a century before. More than likely, this little boy had been a patient. He liked me; I understood his wanderings there. He liked to play with the lights in my office. Sometimes, class attendees saw him and would ask who the little boy was standing next to them. Once, a well-respected paranormal researcher came to my office to give a presentation. I told him how my friend liked to play with the lights. At that precise moment, the lights in my office flickered on and off. The researcher's face turned a shade of white. Once, during a workshop, one of my students saw a little boy in the room. I asked him to say hello. There was a loud knock on the door. I got up to answer and no one was there. It was so nice to see him answer in front of a room full of witnesses.

My late night encounter, however, was much more unsettling. I knew there was a dark spirit that lingered in the hallway of my office. There was a dark passageway that ran alongside, and many mediums had told me they had seen this dark man standing there. So, closing my office at night was always done most quickly. I was on the second floor. There was an inner hallway with a door and then the outside door.

On this night, I locked my office, went down the stairs, and opened the inner door. Looking in through the outside door was a man straight out of Tolkien. He had extremely long, grey hair and an extremely long, grey beard. He was dressed as a wanderer. What scared me most was the vacant expression in his eyes. There was no startle, no *sorry I scared you*...he just looked directly in my eyes without any expression of human recognition.

I quickly closed the inner door, locked it, and ran back upstairs in the dark to my office. I waited for a while in the darkness; it seemed like an eternity. Then, I decided I had better get home before it got any later. I opened the inner door and did not see him. I quickly opened the outer door, locked it, and started walking to my car.

In order to get to my car, I had to pass another front entrance on the opposite side of the building. I saw him again, looking in that door, the same as he had done to mine. Then, my throat sank into my heart as he turned and looked directly at me. I was halfway to the car, halfway from my office. In that moment, I knew a decision must be made. I decided to walk very quickly to my car. I walked on; he stayed at the door just watching.

I don't know who he was, where he belonged, or out of what century he had wandered. I just know I will never forget those vacant eyes. I made it a point to never spend a late night at the office by myself again.

I hope one day to meet a wandering soldier on the battlefield. The first thing I will do is look into his eyes.

Haunting In and About Town

If you have never visited Gettysburg before, there are a few places where I have encountered paranormal

phenomena. One is Sach's Bridge. It is a little out of the way but worth the visit. I have never felt an ominous presence there myself, but I have captured some strange light anomalies and moving orbs at the bridge.

Devil's Den is a very energetic place. It never fails that my camera batteries, though new, will "die" at Devil's Den. It is always frustrating, but I have come to expect it to happen among these boulders that saw so much death.

Farnsworth House is very haunted. As I mentioned earlier, I had the privilege of holding a ghost tour and séance there. Many unexplainable things happened; attendees heard whistles, were touched, and had personal messages revealed during our séance. I have had my hair played with at Farnsworth—there is a spirit there partial to ladies' tresses—

and I have encountered the fragrance of roses in the air, something many at Farnsworth sense.

Cashtown Inn is very well known; it is located in Cashtown, Pennsylvania, not far from Gettysburg. The basement there is very haunted. It was the scene of horrific suffering and amputations. A stream runs through the basement; water intensifies spirit energy. It is here at Cashtown Inn that I have recorded startling Electronic Voice Phenomenon, or EVP. On tape, you can clearly hear a dying soldier's last gasps of breath.

The Grove is a site of one of my most extraordinary photo captures. In one camera shot, the tree is empty. In the next shot, a wispy presence appeared. Seconds later, it vanished in the camera shot. Many large orbs are easy to capture in the Grove. It is the place I feel  the most uneasy at night in all of Gettysburg.

Battlefield Park has strict hours; you cannot wander around there at night. But sometimes, on the back roads of Gettysburg, ghostly apparitions have appeared to startled travelers. Perhaps one day, I will come face-to-face with a wandering soldier.

I like to photograph trees. I find that battlefield trees store wisdom about much that we don't understand and see. Once, I saw the clear face of a soldier etched in a dead tree trunk through my camera lens and on my camera screen. When I got home and uploaded the picture to my computer, his clarity had vanished.

Soldiers' National Cemetery is one of my favorite tree places. One large evergreen seems to weep a purple-colored sap. It is quite beautiful, like amethysts. Another poignant tree bears the perfect shape of a horse etched on its trunk. You can clearly see the eye and nostril and make out the outline of the mane and ears and jaw. He keeps loyal vigil there,  perhaps waiting for his rider to come back to him.

I often find orbs around trees. There are several extremely haunted trees in Gettysburg where orbs often linger. Beside a tree at the Grove, I captured the rising mist with wispy curls that looks like a "little Casper." I have captured various colors and different designs in light anomalies, as well. Many believe orbs are dust or flying insects. I can only speak for many hours of taking pictures, both inside and outdoors. You start to see differences in the ways orbs and night insects move. When you photograph twenty shots of the same view and one contains a strange phenomenon that disappears as quickly as it came, you begin to wonder.

I have led ghost tours and discovered a fascinating phenomenon. If I asked the spirits to show themselves, an orb would appear immediately after. If I told the spirits I was leaving and they had only a few moments left to speak with me, an orb would appear. I have taken videos of moving orbs. One video features me asking the spirits on Sach's Bridge to show themselves, and an immediate orb sails across the screen. I have several videos where I can be heard asking the spirits to appear immediately before the light anomaly, or orb, appears.

Another haunting place to visit is a small, out-of-the-way cemetery that stands next to Barlow's Knoll in Gettysburg National Military Park. It is a tiny spot, but it holds such forceful energy. It is called Alms House Cemetery, where Alms House, a boarding home for the indigent, stood. It was a refuge for the poor and mentally unstable. It is no wonder that those who wandered during life still wander after death.

I feel so many spirits tied to this place. There are no fancy stones or markers; some are simply marked "Unknown Man." How very sad, to lie buried without even your name to mark your time on earth and the passage of your spirit into death. In the off-season, old barren trees stand beside the forgotten inhabitants, large woodchuck holes dug open at their roots. These holes seem to open up the ground for restless spirit passage into the night.

Most paranormal researchers believe cemeteries are not the most energetic places for hauntings. Rather, spirits wander back to places where they lived or where they took their final breaths. So much of the hallowed ground in Gettysburg has been covered with death and sorrow, it is impossible to find an area untouched by 1863. To this day, we still don't know how many are buried yet unaccounted for, how many fragments of bone and relics of battle remain waiting to be found. Perhaps Southern soldiers long to rest once again in soil below the Mason-Dixon line, next to parents and wives and children long at rest. Perhaps parents who never learned the final moments and fates of their beloved sons search the grounds of Gettysburg to this day.

It is extremely windy in Gettysburg. I believe that the most haunted places are often the windiest. The winds seem to carry the energy of restless souls amidst the air. You can often hear the Gettysburg winds howling across the hills. If you ever visit Gettysburg, listen to the wind—it may be whispering a forgotten name or howling with tortured cries of suffering souls.

Part Four

Spirit Energy

Sparky

Some friends call me Sparky, partly because of the Reiki energy, partly because of my relationship with electricity, and partly because of the fact that I can read auras. Our bodies are energy; I can sense the shifts and surges in an aura like a voltage meter can read a battery charge. This can have its downsides. I pop a lot of light bulbs in my house, which can be expensive.

If I am emotionally agitated or angry, things can happen. A toaster once exploded when I came down to breakfast in not the best of moods. A nightlight has exploded in my hands. A heater sparked and exploded in my bathroom. Computers and I sometimes don't have the best of relationships.

I myself had a close encounter with electricity when I was nearly electrocuted as a young woman. Don't for one minute ever think that electrocution is an easy death. I can tell you, it isn't. As electricity travels through your system, you can feel it and hear it make a sound that I can only say closely resembles the sound of a metal drain snake. Your whole body is paralyzed; you cannot move or blink. You are nailed to the ground but fully conscious of this energy coursing through you. You can feel it wrap around your heart.

You cannot scream. My life was spared when the metal chain holding the current broke. Why it broke is not explainable. Perhaps my guardian angel or guide knew I had more to accomplish in life and snapped the metal piece away from my hands.

Whatever divine intervention took place that day will be forever held in gratitude by me and my family. My children would never have been born, these book pages would never have been written. It has left me with a kindred relationship to the powerful electrical energy that fills our Universe and has helped assist me in the path the Universe has chosen.

I am thankful that whatever this energy left behind has given me a heightened ability to connect with unseen energies around me. We all have this ability; I just feel mine has been given a boost.

When I taught classes in psychic development, I always told my students the same thing. Everyone can draw a picture. Some may draw a stick figure, others may draw the Mona Lisa, but we all have the ability to draw. It is the same with intuitiveness; we all possess the ability. Some have it more than others, but it is a gift our souls all possess. We just have to turn the key to access it—or flip on the electrical switch.

Sending Spirits to the Light

Most ghost shows involve sending the spirit "into the light." Some sensitives think it their mission to send every earthbound spirit there.

My thoughts differ. If a spirit is unhappy and causing disruption to his environment, then a discussion of heading toward the light is appropriate. But many spirits are perfectly happy to remain...to remain in the homes they loved, to wander the fields they remember, to sit in the vintage autos that still wait silently in some collectors' garages. If they are happy, then so be it.

I have never been "to the light," though a close call with electricity almost lit up that direction for me. Who am I to tell a spirit that it is better there for him or her? Maybe he or she is happiest here. And most spirits cause no harm to anyone; they wish only to occupy a fleeting space in the atmosphere, a momentary shadow, a lingering mist to visit familiar memories.

That is why times of renovation usually bring spirit activity to a home or building. Spirits like things left as they are. Peeling off great-grandma's favorite wallpaper or updating her very old-fashioned kitchen could be very distressing to her spirit. She will try to communicate this to the owners. Oftentimes, when you hear of paranormal occurrences in a home, it is shortly after some major renovation project. Spirits like things the way they were, the way they remember them.

I have led ghost investigations and held séances in both Gettysburg and New Jersey. These are not done as parlor games, but rather as modes of respectful communication between planes of existence. Perhaps it was my prior bout with electricity that heightened my sensitivity to the energies that are unseen but always around us.

There is dark energy about. One must learn ways to communicate and protect, for if a spirit is not peaceful, there are three scenarios:

He or she can remain in a state of unrest.

He or she can move "into the light."

He or she can follow you home.

If a spirit is trapped on this plane, and venturing toward the light is not a present option, the only way he or she can move away from the entrapment is to use you as a vehicle. This, you do not want.

A simple way to protect yourself if ever faced with a darker energy is to remember that the light will protect. Surround yourself with it. Call on whichever energies you hold uppermost in prayers—the Universe, Angels, spirit guides,

Jesus—they will help you return home without an unwanted presence beside you.

Gettysburg is a town filled with antiques and relics, and there are numerous places to purchase such items. Always remember, inanimate objects hold residual energy. I often worry about someone purchasing an item and having its previous owner accompanying him or her back home. Just as that vintage car I spoke of earlier may have an unseen driver, that vintage locket from the 19th century may bring the energy of its previous owner to your door.

As a Reiki Master, I learned ways to clear the energy from people and objects. A simple method is just to say a blessing when you purchase any object once belonging to another. This method can apply to garage sale, estate sale, and flea market finds, as well. Anytime you feel the energy of something is not right, pass it by...it might be your intuition feeling the lingering presence of something *dark*.

There have been a couple of instances where an unfamiliar spirit has hitched a ride into my home. My dogs will act differently, refusing to climb the stairs. My CD player will turn on or the alarm clock will ring. Usually, the visit is short-lived. Spirits must like to take vacations, too. Usually by the week's end, the dogs are climbing the stairs again and all is back to *normal.*

Dark Energy

I was raised in a culture ingrained with superstitions and rituals; I could not escape the knowledge of these beliefs. I have chosen not to pass most on to my children. One of these is the infamous *evil eye*. My mother was one of the few skilled in removing this curse. She didn't choose to share this information with me. She died before she fully knew all the skills her daughter possessed. It was only after her death that I learned she possessed her own gifts and knew most of mine, although I never told her. She chose for me to walk my own path, just as I choose for my children to do the same.

My path has brought me to a different form of cleansing and spreading light. So, in a way, I continue her cleansing of darkness.

Do I believe in curses? I have grown up seeing how these beliefs torment and affect the lives of believers. I do believe there is dark energy and dark intent. But I believe it is our own self doubt (in the ability of our own shields to protect us from this darkness) that causes the most harm. Light will prevail over darkness, but each of us must choose the amount of light we let enter and defend.

Curiosity about the darkness can create small tears in our shields, big enough to let the negative in. This curiosity is what leads inexperienced paranormal enthusiasts and impressionable youths who delve into supernatural subjects astray. Curiosity about the darkness can issue invites to the dark.

If you open the doorways to the supernatural, you must be prepared to lock those doorways so uninvited energies do not gain entrance. If you leave the front door of your home open, a stranger may wander in uninvited. If you leave your intuitive channel open, uninvited energies can wander in, as well.

My one unpleasant experience at the farmhouse happened when I brought a spirit board inside. I have never used one; now, I realize that that has been one of the wisest choices I have made along the path. Perhaps my farmhouse spirits were admonishing me for what they perceived as a tear in my shield. They are at peace at my farm; they didn't want any uninvited, tormented spirits coming to my opened door.

Thoughts, words, and intentions all have energy. We can send them with goodness, or we can send them with evil. In the end, I believe the Universe will bring back to you what it is you chose to put forth along your path.

Do Some Humans Carry Dark Energy?

Being involved in the metaphysical field has brought some sad and tormented souls to my office, living souls whose daily lives are affected by mysterious, troubling, and unexplainable occurrences.

One such soul was a woman who started coming to my office, attending workshops, and calling me on the phone for guidance. She was an extremely troubled soul, searching for answers, answers I could not give. She, too, had found most comfort living an isolated life, experiencing short moments of happiness feeding the birds and squirrels outside her window. Poltergeist activity was commonplace in her home. Her own body was a magnet for paranormal and metaphysical anomalies. She could not wear a watch; she kept it in her purse. She demonstrated why by putting it on her wrist. The hands of the watch moved furiously about as if she, herself, was the quartz crystal affecting movement.

For these reasons, she was a big distraction at workshops. The fluorescent lights in my office reacted strangely by buzzing loudly when she took a seat under them. This scared the other attendees to the point that her presence was becoming an issue. The more I tried to politely avoid her contact, the more she persisted in showing up at my office unannounced.

I felt sorry for her, but this woman so affected my own energy that I could no longer be near her. Even a phone call from her could shake my whole energy system—and not in a beneficial way. If she had ever asked me to do Reiki on her, I would have refused. There was something very powerful and affecting about her presence, I knew I must keep as much distance between her and me as possible.

One evening, late at night, as I was about to close my office, I realized that I could not find my key. I did not like being alone at the office after dark for reasons mentioned earlier. I did not carry a cell phone, but luckily, the therapist in the office beneath me was having a late session. She must have thought I needed a therapy session myself, as I knocked and entered at such an hour, asking to use her phone. I never installed a phone at my Reiki office. Thinking back now, I should have; I had a couple of close calls with clients interested in more than a metaphysical chakra alignment.

I called my best friend and former business partner. Thankfully, she still kept her office key. Now, I didn't mention the most mysterious event of this night. Parked outside my office was the car belonging to the woman with the strange energy. She usually went to the diner across the street and then would stop in my office to see what events were posted in the hallway. I did not want to run into this woman, even more so now that I was trapped in my office space and could not go home.

My friend could tell what a rattled state I was in. She knew about this woman. I told her on the phone that she was parked out front. My friend came quickly and *rescued* me.

She mentioned that she had walked past the car out front and took note of the license plate. In New Jersey, we have letters and numbers on our plates. This woman's plate read KEY...

Sometimes, you don't have to travel to the Twilight Zone—the zone comes looking for you.

Part Five

Past Lives

Glimpses of My Past

Ever since I was a little girl, I have experienced "moments from my past." They are hard to describe unless you have experienced them. It is not the same as walking into a room and knowing you have been there before; these are actual buried memories inside my head.

I remember one vivid voice, a cruel voice. I would hear it every so often in my mind as a kid. When the memory was over, try as I might, I could never duplicate the sound of that voice in my head. It was only there for that moment. Then, it was gone.

I have had many past lives; I am an old soul. My past lives weren't happy ones. I was imprisoned or worse for the things that I could do or for who I was. I won't go into all here, but there are a few memories I wish to share.

I have dreams of past lives—not dreams, but windows into time. One takes place in ancient Rome. I am near the Coliseum. There are two important images in this dream. One is an old woman, hunched over and dressed completely in black. She is pushing, or at least attempting to push, a wagon or cart or wheelbarrow of some kind. Inside the cart is a shrouded body. Romans are jeering and taunting her every step on this arduous journey. She is compelled to make it to her destination. I feel it is a journey to put this body to proper rest.

Some years ago, I was privileged to be regressed by Brian Weiss, the most respected researcher in this field. Past life regression is a wondrous thing. I have witnessed many at my former office, some expected and others that took my breath away for their truth and authenticity. I felt like I was under for hours, but in reality, it was about thirty minutes. At first, the importance of what I saw did not register. Being regressed is such a profound experience; it takes time to fully understand what has occurred. I was led to viewing rooms or passages to see my past lives. In one of those rooms, I saw an old woman in black being stoned to death. I had always thought I was the shrouded body. Thanks to Brian Weiss, I learned that I was the mother—a mother desperately trying to bring her child to rest.

I think that this is the whole reason for my connection to the dying, my reverence for the honor and upkeep of cemeteries, and my interest (as a taphophile) in photographing cemetery statues and architecture. And also my connection to Elizabeth Thorn of Evergreen Cemetery.

* I have two daughters. Many years ago, when my youngest was in high school and my eldest was in college, I took them to

Italy. One afternoon, in Rome, we were taking photos in a piazza across from the Pantheon. My daughters had cameras, but I didn't, so I do not have a picture. (I believe that is as this story should be—pictureless, a moment envisioned in the reader's mind.) At the entrance to the Pantheon, I saw a stooped figure, hunched back, bent with the ravages of a hard life. She was covered in black from head to toe. I watched as she begged for change as each tourist passed her outstretched hands. I could not see her face; she was too far away. I am glad, for the silhouette of her presence has haunted me enough through these years. I saw so many magnificent things in Italy—the Sistine Chapel, the Grand Canal in Venice, the cathedrals of Florence—but, a hunchbacked crone, dressed in black, is the one that haunts my mind and memory most vividly.

"A Horse and a Garnet"

He carved for days……
Each detail of the mane, the ears, the hooves
A master of his craft
Take it……
His hand extended to his wife and baby…….
Remember me…..

No…..

We will remember, and wait

You take it…….

He will protect you and carry you home

Hidden in a little tasseled pouch

A small horse for strength

A garnet for protection

A shield and tunic covering both

Long marches

Tired bones

Spirits whittled like his horse amulet

Tired eyes glazed red

Like the glow of a garnet

Each night

Under stars

A weathered hand clasps each

Remembering……..

The reign of trumpets

The storms of rain

Cries of pain

A Roman General

Looking out upon his legion

Bodies strewn across the field

How will I forget

There are so many

Drops of rain soak his tunic

Drops of blood soak his

Weathered hands

Still clasping a horse

To carry him home

And Garnet

Dark as blood

To protect him on his journey

To Elysian Fields

Do not

Forget

Me...........

My Earliest Past

My most ancient time on earth was as a healer, a wise crone. Perhaps that is what has led me to this healing path in present time. I looked much like myself, except for curly tendrils, not straight lengths of hair. I was persecuted by those who feared me. I lived a life shunned by humans; instead, I dwelled among animal companions, cherished and connected with the world of nature and animal familiars.

My past life memory is a very sad one. Usually, these memories that survive reveal traumatic moments. Mine was the moment when those who feared me hurt me in a way worse than burning or hanging. In my visions, I had birds. I lived among large raptors, hawks, and falcons that perched on my shoulders and communicated with me in mysterious, misunderstood ways. It was the moment all of my animals were killed in front of my eyes that has stayed in my soul for centuries. That hurt has lingered and has never healed. I believe it forged the healing path my soul has chosen for me now. It could also be the reason why many birds share my home and life today.

Past lives have such a strong influence on who we currently are, what we fear, and what we are drawn to in this lifetime. The past is never far behind; it waits within our souls behind a locked door. Some of us find the key that opens it; some never do.

When I first became interested in Celtic/Druidic astrology, I learned that our time of birth can provide a glimpse into that door. Many of those for whom I have done astrological profiles have remarked how precisely the past life information fits—fits their fears, their struggles, and the secrets of their souls.

"Sun and Sand"

A little boy
Sitting in the sand
Ocean's edge
Gazing at the sun
Amidst the waves
Sparkling in the foam

His mother
Sitting beside
Hand extended toward
The sun
Catching rainbows
In
Her diamond's sunburst

A young man racing by

Kicking up sand

Sun rays gleaming

Against the metal chain

Binding his dog to him

Racing alongside

An old woman

Slowly shuffling by

Disrupting the sand

Her walker

Pushing tediously onward

Its handles glistening in the sunlight

A young mother

Staring at the

Golden Handles

Of a Casket

Gleaming in the morning sun

Her little boy

By her side

Staring at the dewdrop

On a blade of grass

Shimmering in the sunlight

Parents sitting under the shield

Of a cemetery tent

Their *son's light* forever

Vanished by the shadow

Of the sands of time

"Walking Past"

I watch, from my window….

He is here again…

Walking past my door

Where he belongs….

Like the first, fragile snowdrop

Peering up from melting snows

Or the first brave redbreast

Pecking for hibernating worms

His Lincolnesque stride, tall and wiry

A weary countenance that never waivers,

Never meets mine….

Only looking forward to the next steps on his journey

Steps I feel are filled with loneliness….

I watch him year to year

Long overcoat buttoned against the winds

Knitted cap pulled down over sullen eyes

I wonder

Where he goes…….

Perhaps to a daughter who waits

I hope, but think not…

For if I were his daughter

 I would not let him wander the cold pavements…

Sometimes, I see him as I drive by

And am tempted to say,

"Need a ride?"

But no…..

For he is right where he belongs….

And I am where I belong….

Each in our own space in the Universe

Following our paths…..

Winter, Summer

Rain, Sun

He is there……..

One afternoon, several miles from home,

I saw him walking

Such distance for an old man

It made me all the more curious

Then, I saw him no more….

Vanished, my walking ghost

Haunting my pavements and curiosity no more…….

I looked and looked…….

Sometimes, to this day, I still look

Though I know his earthly walk is no longer possible

Perhaps one day, when I take my final walk

I will see him…….

This time, I will catch up and say "hello"

For I always felt his loneliness pass by

He never knew a young woman thought of him

Each time he passed her door

I hope his destination led to rest

For his weary legs

And love

For his weary soul.

A Voice from the Tower

I have had other glimpses into my past. I think I lived similar lives in distant times, times where the work I do would have been a danger to my existence. And I think I paid with my life because of it.

I have always known that the work I do would have led me to the fiery stake in other centuries. I feel that path has been one traveled.

I love visiting England. I have captured many orbs in photographs, and I have captured one very poignant EVP session at the Tower of London. EVP is Electronic Voice Phenomenon. A tape recorder can sometimes pick up things inaudible to our ears at the time of the recording.

While at the Tower, I entered the dungeon cell of Anne Askew, a woman who was tortured on the rack and burned at the stake because of religious witch hunts. Anne was an English poet and Protestant. She is the only known woman on record to be tortured and then burned at the Tower. Anne was tortured so horrendously, her body was literally torn apart, bones dislocated and joints separated.

As I entered her cell, I asked her to speak to me. It was years before I finally listened to all of my recording sessions. To my amazement, in Anne's cell, the distinctive voice of a woman can be heard telling me to *listen.* (If you are intrigued, my EVP sessions can be accessed on my blog page.)

The day after I heard this recording, I was very badly burned on my entire forearm in a kitchen accident. My burn healed much better than anyone ever imagined; there is only a slight discoloration on my skin. But Anne's mark on my memory will forever remain.

I think Anne desperately needed someone to finally listen to her voice. Perhaps we had a personal connection through the centuries; she chose to call out to a kindred spirit.

Unforgettable Regressions

A troubled, middle-aged man once came to my office for Past Life Regression. He was troubled in this life, addicted to ways to soothe his tortured soul.

He told me that as a kid, he had been running down the street and accidentally bumped into an elderly woman. She fell and subsequently died from that fall. He had spent his life looking for ways to drown out that guilt. He wanted to be regressed; he had read that it sometimes brought demons to light. Maybe it could help him.

Under regression, we went back to days of the Old West. He described an isolated fort, the people gravely in need of supplies. He was the wagon driver bringing in those supplies. At the fort, there was a horrible accident—a child was run over by the wagon horses and killed. He carried the death of that child with him for centuries, so much so that his soul chose to repeat the trauma in hopes to finally bring reconciliation and peace from the lesson.

If we do not reach peace, our mistakes will return to us. They will come in another lifetime and another.

I always wondered what became of that man after he left the regression.

Another regression was done on a mother and daughter. The daughter had been plagued by nightmares, dreams of wandering through a forest, searching frantically for something or someone. Her regression revealed much the same—searching through woods, frantic searching.

The mother was then regressed. She had lost a child in a previous lifetime. Could the child now in her present lifetime carry similar memories that plagued her sleepless nights to this day? I think they realized they had finally found each other after the regressions. Maybe both could be a little more at peace now.

Of course, I have witnessed the usual regressions, of people burning at the stake or honored as some ancient Royal. But, it is the above regressions, the emotional memories, that linger in my mind. Watching a mother crying over a baby lost to sickness, seeing a father tell his son his dying wishes—these are the regressions that I will never forget.

Your Past Will Find You

As a teen, I collected snoods. I had one in every color. I used to wear them around my hair, which I wrapped in a bun. A bun hairstyle for a teen—that alone should give you a clue that I am an ancient soul.

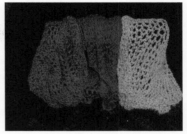

Snoods are popular in Gettysburg. Waitresses in inns wear them, ghost tour guides wear them, costumed reenactors wear them. It is not unusual to see snoods sold in shops all across town.

Once, I told my best friend in adult life about my snoods, and she couldn't believe it. One day, smashed into the sidewalk in front of the office at which we both worked, was an old, black snood. I really wanted to pick it up, but something made me leave it. It haunted me; for years, I would remember it.

This happened long before I first visited Gettysburg. I had always wanted to go there, but the time wasn't right. I guess the time for bringing old snoods back into my life wasn't right yet either.

When I purchased my farmhouse, I commenced shopping at thrift stores and antique shops. You find some wonderful things there, things that fit perfectly into an old farmhouse. One day, I bought a small, wooden jewelry box. When I opened the drawer, a black snood was waiting. I guess it was time.

Yes, your past will find you when the time is right. Sometimes, you get a little preview. If you don't answer, it will come back one day.

Gazing into Familiar Eyes

I collect daguerreotypes, Civil War Era photographs. I have had many unusual paranormal experiences with dags (as they are called). I seem to have a gift for finding people in them; friends and family in my present are often found in the faces of the 1800s.

One day, I found myself. I gazed into a daguerreotype and saw my own eyes looking back at me. It is an unexplainable feeling.

Coincidentally, I found the best friend I just spoke of shortly thereafter.

The likeness is unquestionable, an exact double. I have also found a couple of her good friends.

Once, I brought in a print of a daguerreotype to the office. It looked exactly like one of her very close friends. I showed it to her and asked her who it looked like. She hesitated but then said it was me, although something was not *right*. She quickly left the room with this print. I found her at the copy machine, quickly trying to make a duplicate. I asked again, "Now who does this look like?" With much unease and disbelief, she said it was her friend. I had only met her friend once, long before. She couldn't believe how I would still recognize her and *find* her this way. I was so happy she saw it, too, and that I wasn't crazy. I remember just hugging her there in the copy room.

We have all been together before. Souls find each other through each lifetime and journey as friends, as spouses, as siblings, or as enemies—however the Universe deems appropriate for karmic lessons.

Once, while gazing at my computer in a file of these personal daguerreotypes, I asked to be led to some answers about my past. The television was turned on in the living room to some obscure station. All of a sudden, scenes of the Battle of Gettysburg played across the TV in some little known documentary series I have yet to find again. Running into the living room and seeing my TV screen was a spine-chilling experience.   I think the spirits of my past were coming through—and they used modern technology to do so.

The Woman in the Picture

On my first visit to Gettysburg, we visited the Farnsworth House. There used to be a bookstore in the lower level where one could purchase prints, souvenirs, and, of course, books.

Wandering down the book aisles, I saw a print on the wall. I cannot explain it, but the feeling from this print was so overwhelming, I literally had to take a few moments to compose myself. We left the store, but like the snood, this print haunted me.

On our second visit to Gettysburg, we went back to Farnsworth. I bought this print. I still had no idea who this

 pregnant woman holding a digging spade in her hands was yet. We didn't know our way around town that well or all historic facts about Gettysburg yet; we were learning by exploring and driving around. We visited Soldiers' National Cemetery, a place where most seek to honor.

We drove up the wrong drive to Evergreen Cemetery. As we entered through the gatehouse, I saw the woman in my print—the sculpture of Elizabeth.

Sometimes, strange twinges of remembrance overtake us, feelings that we have some connection, that there is some purpose for our reunions in life. I read all I could get my hands on about Elizabeth. Her daughter was called Rose, a name that undoubtedly connects to her last name, and a name that is of great importance to me. My Wordpress blog is called *The Roses and Thorns of Life.* Rose is my own middle name, my business name, and my mother's name.

I have always had a reverence and love for cemeteries, and I have always felt a responsibility to care for the dying and buried. Could this be my connection to her?

During my extensive search, I found the daguerreotype of Elizabeth Thorn. I will not print it here, for it is not mine to publish. But, if you should have an interest, do an Internet search for the face of Elizabeth….she looks a lot like me.

I feel some connection with this woman. Perhaps what it is will remain a mystery from the past. I only know how I feel when I see her face above me as I sit at my oak writing desk at the farmhouse. Perhaps she is content to watch me write these words.

I have taken many pictures at Evergreen, especially with Elizabeth.

Many show an orb around us. Maybe the orb is of a very brave woman, now at rest, with an energy that still connects to mine in a mysterious way.

By the way, we tried to get dinner reservations for Cashtown that evening, but it was closed. Our innkeepers suggested an out-of-the-way place, just across the Maryland border, called the Carriage House. We had a wonderful dinner there, and among the photographs on the wall were pictures of a dinner held to honor the statue unveiling of one heroic, pregnant woman in Gettysburg, 1863. After dinner, the waitress handed me a rose...

There are no coincidences, only messages from other places of existence.

My Husband's Daguerreotype

My husband and I like Mackinac Island, Michigan. If you have seen the movie *Somewhere in Time*, you know the place of which I speak. The movie concerns time travel, a subject close to my heart since childhood days of reading Jules Verne. The movie soundtrack itself is quite haunting, composed by Rachmaninoff and John Barry.

While searching through antique dag websites, I came upon one that looked very much like my husband. The page had music attached—the music from *Somewhere in Time*. As I read through the information on the dag, one of those neck hair-raising moments arose. The dag had been dug up from—

well, I think you know my next words. Yes, Mackinac Island, Michigan. Now my dag and his are together again.

Coincidence, fate, past lives—you decide.

Gettysburg in the Blood

Some have Gettysburg in their blood; it's an affliction not easily explained. It explains the yearly return trips and the obsession with Gettysburg movies, books, reenactments, and battlegrounds.

Some sense a connection with the past, a feeling that their feet have walked across a certain ground in a time before.

I have three children born with this *connection.* My youngest daughter's birthday is also the anniversary of Gettysburg's first day of battle. My son's birthday is shared with General Ulysses S. Grant. My eldest daughter's birth was not on a day associated with Gettysburg, but a couple of years ago, she brought a son-in-law into our family. He shares the same birthday as my son.

Some may say it is mere coincidence. Me, I am sticking to my story...Gettysburg is in some families' blood.

Part Six

Angels

A Good Friday Angel

ast night's dream was the impetus for this early morning chapter. I dreamt of Michael Landon, dressed as a priest, beckoning me back to church. Logically, I know the reason. I have been enjoying daily reruns of *Highway to Heaven* each afternoon at five o'clock. This week was the episode where Jonathan and Mark assume the identities of priests to bring a lonely, young couple together.

I always loved Michael Landon. Ironically, the very last picture taken of my mom shows a newspaper headline that reads, "Michael Landon dies." My mom died very soon after. Each time I look at that photo, it is very bittersweet. Three humans, so important to my heart, now gone—my mom, my young niece (whom I wrote of in my first book), and Michael.

I was raised Roman Catholic. My church is filled with saints and Vatican rules. For several years, I volunteered to teach very young children as a Catechist. I like to think that I made a lasting impression on each life. I would tell them of miraculous happenings in the world, documented by witnesses, such as the mysterious miracles of Saint Anthony and Padre Pio. I would delight them with tales of Saint Joseph of Copertino, the flying monk. The Church has such unexplainable stories; they always fascinated me. I left that formal church many years ago, but I never left those saints, those stories, or my faith.

Now, my moments in church are spent alone, usually on Feast or Saints' Days, when the church is still left unlocked. I like to sit alone, not among rows of parishioners where I never felt comfortable. The only day I will go to Mass is on Saint Francis' Day for the Blessing of the Animals. I go to the Cathedral of St. John the Divine in New York City. If you are ever near during this October celebration, it is something you should witness at least once.

One Good Friday, almost a decade ago, I had a longing to go back to church. It was late afternoon; I knew the church doors would be locked soon, so I hurried over to light a candle and say a prayer at the statue of Jesus and his grieving mother. The neighborhood church, like most others nowadays, has electric candles for safety purposes. But on Good Friday, a special altar of flame burning candles is set up. (I miss those candles from childhood and the wonder of lighting them. You just don't get the same impression from pressing an electric button.)

When I walked into the church, it was deserted. I entered the vestibule, where the candles were lit, and put my offering in the candle box. I knelt at the candle altar, picked out an unlit one, and reached for the long sticks to light it.

(For those of you unfamiliar, long sticks are arranged in a container of sand. You pick one, light your candle, and safely put it back in the container.) The stick container was empty.

I searched and searched frantically for a way to light my candle. I don't smoke, so I had no lighter or matches. As I feared that the doom of eternity would be on me if I couldn't accomplish this feat, I saw a container of tiny pencils next to the entry book. I tried to light a pencil; thankfully, it didn't work. I might have had a real fire on my hands if it did.

I sat there mournfully, alone, in this deserted church on a Good Friday, unable to light a candle to the Lord.

Suddenly, out of nowhere, a man appeared at the candles. I am not the type of person who asks strangers in deserted places for any sort of help, but I heard myself saying, "Do you have a match?" This man smiled. I don't remember his face, but I remember his smile. He handed me a matchbook.

Now, I have always had problems lighting matches. Fire is a karmic issue I carry from centuries past. I opened the matchbook, and there was only ONE match. I always have such a difficult time lighting matches; I knew this would be my only shot. I struck it, and it lit. When I turned around to thank him and offer him his empty matchbook back, he was gone.

I took a moment to digest what had just happened. I looked down at the matchbook in my hand. On the cover was a yellow rose. You have read before of the importance of roses in my life—my mother's name, my middle name, my business name. So much of my present and past is entangled with roses. There was a series of numbers on the matchbook...the numbers of my birth date.

I kept that matchbook. I think a Good Friday Angel gave it to me so I could light a candle to the Lord.

You Never Know When an Angel Is Passing By

Many, many years ago, I was in my front yard with my three young children in tow. I was in a very sullen mood; we had just lost a bid on what I thought was my "dream house." I used to sit outside this house waiting for my eldest to come out of preschool, imaging myself living there. When it went on the market, I was thrilled. We put a bid on it. Although our bid was higher, another bid had been placed and verbally accepted earlier, and the owner, afraid of legal repercussions, declined ours. I was heartsick. I still remember crying in bed that night.

Life goes on, though. My children and I were tending to some garden work out front the next day. I was still in my miserable mood.

A tiny, old woman with a silvery bun walked along the sidewalk. Though I had lived here many years, I had never seen her before. She stopped in front of my house, smiled at me and my three children, and said, "You are blessed to have so much." I never forgot those words or that woman. I have never seen her since. Just an old woman passing by—or an angel to let me "see" how much I really had, not how much I thought I'd lost?

Recently, on a very stormy night, late and weary from traveling from Gettysburg back to New Jersey, another angel appeared in the sky to my husband and me. In spite of the rain and wind, I could not pass by without capturing her with my camera.

Sometimes, Spirits Warn

Many times during Reiki sessions, I will pick up on messages for the client. Energy is so intertwined; the energy of spirits is able to come through to me during my sessions.

One such session involved a young woman. I did not know the girl; it was the first time she had ever come to my office. Yet, I feel that I may have played a small role in keeping her out of harm's way.

During the Reiki session, a message of warning came through. I asked her if she planned on going out that evening. If so, she should be very careful about whose car she was getting into. I relayed to her a warning of intoxication and harm tied to this choice. I do not usually tell people messages like this, but this one was very compelling.

With a frightened look on her face, she answered that she was going to a club that night. She had not seen a friend in a long time. This friend had a bad history of DUIs but had told her she was now on a better path. This friend would be driving that evening.

The girl left my office visibly shaken. My husband was outside waiting in the car for me. He said she immediately got on her cell phone. I hope she called this friend and arranged to do the driving herself.

I never saw this girl again. I think I frightened her. Perhaps that fear saved her from harm, though. She had a guardian spirit watching over her during our session. This spirit perhaps kept her from impending injury.

Part Seven

Cemeteries

Are Cemeteries Haunted?

I like to wander around cemeteries and take photographs. As I roam, I look for little snippets of the heart, touching mementos left at a gravestone or weeds grown to the wind with abandon. Each tells its own story. Finding that moment that I know will transcend into my camera and into your heart is like finding a diamond in the rough.

Each resident is a diamond; some are polished with manicured landscapes, and some are "in the rough," with overgrown weeds and dandelion blossoms adorning their graves. To me, they are all precious jewels of time, shining in the sunlight or waiting in the rain for a taphophile's heart and camera. To me, those dandelion weeds can be more precious than a landscape of perfection. Each sight is perfection, telling a story better than a thousand words. Yes, I love to write stories, but what I love most are the stories that need not be written, the stories in my camera lens.

Some believe that the only spirit to *haunt* a cemetery is the very first body laid to rest. This spirit now becomes the guardian of the cemetery, watching over all the others who follow.

I have never felt harmful energy in the cemeteries I have roamed. I have, though, felt incredible sadness in

Soldiers' National Cemetery. There is a row of soldiers' graves where one particular soldier rests—or rather does not rest. He is mournful; I sense the loss he feels of losing his wife and his daughter, of dying and never watching her grow up.

Animals sometimes lead me to graves in the cemetery. A little rabbit led me to this soldier's grave. If you see an animal in the cemetery, take a photo. Many times, you will capture an orb. Oftentimes, animals act as messengers of the spirit world. If you see one in a haunted location, follow it and see where it leads you.

There is a unique statue in a New Jersey cemetery I like to visit. I call her the Bleeding Angel, as you can see by her picture. Strange blood-colored stains drip from her neck. You can visit her at the Immaculate Conception Cemetery in Upper Montclair, NJ.

Green-wood Cemetery
Listening to the Living and the Dead

Driving through the congested streets of Brooklyn, passing padlocked abandonment and graffitied walls, one's eyes cannot help but be mesmerized by the enchanting gates of Green-wood.

Not an ordinary cemetery, Green-wood is a magical passageway to another plane of existence, or *after existence.* The towering entrance looms overhead, complete with resident wild parrots (and their immense twig nests), squawking high toward Heaven.

Green-wood is a landscape marvel. Beautiful flowers and meticulously manicured specimens of rare, native trees line its paths, and leaf-laden limbs overhang, shielding visitors from the sun as they walk the gravesites. Each tree and bush is kept in optimum condition by a team of dedicated people. Long before parks, cemeteries were the picnic and recreation destinations for the living. Green-wood served as the model for Central Park. Today, it upholds this prestigious distinction; the grounds are breathtakingly beautiful. One can easily imagine formally-dressed Victorians picnicking along the ponds and strolling along the shady, tree-lined walkways of this Brooklyn landmark.

I visit cemeteries to pay reverence to the dead, but I always learn a lot from the living visitors, as well. On one particular visit to Green-wood, I took a two-hour trolley tour of the cemetery grounds. As we meandered along, a guide pointed out the notable stories and impressive array of greenery greeting us along the journey. Spring had come early this year; we missed the dogwoods, but the azaleas more than paid for the loss. If one envisions drab as an adjective for cemeteries, one needs to visit Green-wood on a sunny, spring day.

The trolley made a final stop at the Civil War Monument. Green-wood is the resting place for many nineteenth-century soldiers. At this point, passengers could choose to walk the rest of the path toward the entrance gate or remain seated in the trolley.

I stayed for a time on the trolley, just observing the living and the dead. Like I mentioned, you can learn a lot from each in the cemetery. This day was no exception. Since I own a Civil War farmhouse in Gettysburg, this was a fitting and peaceful spot to sit and observe my surroundings.

Many steps lead up to the Civil War Memorial. The open air trolley was parked right at the base of these steps. I had the perfect vantage point. Standing at the top of the steps was a frail, white-haired man holding a cane.

"Could someone please help me?" he asked.

From the crowd of tourists stepped forward a younger, white-haired version of the questioner. Extending his arm, they descended, hand-in-hand, slowly to the base. I watched and listened...and learned.

The younger gentleman asked the cane-wielding one how old he was. "I am eighty-two," he answered. Then he proceeded to make some light-hearted comment about how people were dying to get in here, and he would soon be one of them. People often make lighthearted jokes about subjects that bring fear to their hearts. The younger one laughed. People often laugh when emotional unease surpasses *correctness.*

"I thought you were just a year older than me," he said with a twinkle in his eye. "I am sixty-five."

The older gent commented that he was a *"youngster."* I am sure this comforted a man facing the fears of his own "dying to get in here" future.

So, hand-in-hand, they both helped each other that sunny, spring afternoon. One helping the other down the steps on the start of his journey, and one telling the other that many more steps still awaited him on his.

You learn a lot about the living and the dead at a cemetery. That afternoon in Green-wood was no exception.

The Cemetery Is Just Like Any Other Neighborhood

I always wished to visit European cemeteries that replicate the villages where their inhabitants now lay buried. Supposedly, walking through one is like walking through a little town.

I think cemeteries are like that, just neighborhoods. Most of the residents are away, exploring other realms and adventures. Some homebodies like to stick around. There are always a few bullies in any neighborhood who like to scare and cause mayhem. On the whole, cemeteries are not places to fear.

I have walked through cemeteries are midnight. Hands are not reaching up from the ground to grab as movies like to portray. If any wanderers are about, perhaps a little orb will show their harmless presence.

My mother crossed many, many years ago. She was buried about half a mile from my home. I would drive by the cemetery on my way to visit my dad. I would visit her every day. It took a long while, but my beliefs changed over time. I grew more and more aware that she was not *there*; I did not have to go anywhere to visit her. She was always with me.

Yes, her grave was a place to adorn, but the true place to visit was within me.

When I photograph cemeteries, they are, for the most part, lonely places. The adornments embellish vacant plots of earth; those visited have traveled on to new journeys and beginnings.

It is a shame we are losing the beautiful statues and grandeur of old cemeteries. Many Angels and Saints are crumbling into dust and ashes, as all our mortal bodies must.

This photo was taken at Sleepy Hollow Cemetery, along the Hudson in upstate New York. It is the famed haunting ground of Washington Irving's Headless Horseman.

Photographic glitches may explain the cause, but perhaps the spirits thought it funny that these orbs should completely cover my face...as if they are talking to me.

Just like in any neighborhood, there are good residents and bad, good energies and bad. And, as Mr. Rogers so kindly asked...one day, we will all be neighbors.

Part Eight

Paranormal Photographs from Around the World

Caroline

Amidst the tangled ivy and brittle leaves of Highgate Cemetery in London stands the poignant statue for Caroline. Quite serene and beautiful, her presence fills visitors with a sense of peace. I captured a beautiful orb at Caroline's grave, its brilliance as bright as the peaceful aura around her memorial.

Highgate is quite an extraordinary place, from tales of grave robbers to not-so-distant sightings of the legendary "Highgate Vampire." If you journey to London, make sure to give this haunted place a spot on your travel checklist.

I took this photo at Highgate Cemetery in London. Above this poignant statue, a most beautiful orb appeared on film......I have not retuched or photo-shopped this picture in any way.

Casper at the Grove

Next to the Gettysburg Middle School stands a piece of ground saturated with torment, bloodied by one of the most brutal confrontations in 1863. So brutal, that when ammunition was depleted, soldiers fought with the disembodied limbs of the fallen. Here is where a little wisp of a spirit visited me. In an instant, he was floating beside the tree. In the next instant, he was gone. I call him Casper; his little curly wisp reminds me of a beloved childhood ghost.

Dobbin House Anomaly

The Dobbin House in Gettysburg dates back to the 18th century. Its original tavern is still a well-loved place to enjoy good food and drink among friends. Having been built in 1776, it is Gettysburg's oldest standing structure, and it has seen a lot of trauma and history pass by and through its doors.

I attended a paranormal dinner at Dobbin House a few years ago. Richard Felix, a well-respected historian from the United Kingdom, was giving a presentation. As the evening wound down to a close, I stopped to chat with Richard, and my husband snapped this picture.

Above the head of a woman dressed in period costume is a unique paranormal anomaly. We showed it to many paranormal investigators, and each one could offer no explainable reason for such a shape. We still don't have an answer as to who was crashing the dinner presentation that night.

The Reaper Tree

I like to photograph trees. I think they shelter and nourish the energy of spirits. In Immaculate Conception Cemetery, the same home to the Bleeding Angel, I found this tree. There seems to be a reaper peering around the trunk, scythe in hand, beckoning visitors to not fear him.

The Keyhole Tree

I believe trees hold spirit energy. Sometimes, the trees themselves are potent doorways to energy. There is one such tree in Immaculate Conception Cemetery. I call her the Keyhole Tree; it looks as though her trunk holds portal to another dimension.

Trees have witnessed so much and store so much wisdom in their trunks. To me, it is no wonder that they hold such powerful energy sources, as well.

The Crucifixion Tree

At Holy Cross Cemetery in New Jersey stands a tree long drained of any living energy. Its lifeless trunk holds another type of energy—spiritual energy. The moment I saw this tree, I saw him. Rather, I saw Him on the Cross. His crucified body was all I could see against the sky.

Each time I visit this cemetery, I walk to him. I breathe a sigh of relief when I see him standing there. I know that one day, cemetery workers will cut this trunk down, never realizing how special it is. Until that day, each time I walk the grounds of Holy Cross, I walk toward him.

Light Anomalies and Orbs

I have captured many light anomalies and shapes that have even baffled paranormal experts. I have included some in the last chapter of this section.

If you wish to capture spirits or orbs in photos, the key is taking several shots in quick succession. The first photo may be empty, the second may show an anomaly, and the third may return to normal again. It is a little bit of luck, as well. I shoot hundred of pictures—you learn to identify which are orbs, which are dust, and which are bugs.

This brilliant orb appeared during a midnight walk on Hallween night at Sleepy Hollow Cemetery. There was no source of light other than our hand held lanterns...

I have been lucky enough to capture a few orbs in motion. One of my most fascinating catches was taken right inside my porch door. There was no dust, and since it was the dead of winter, no bugs out freezing their little behinds off. You can clearly see the orb in motion in my photograph. It is completely unexplainable. Even more unexplainable is the

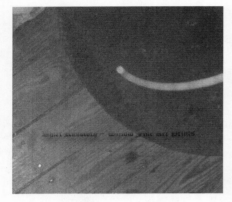

fact that I had mistakenly pressed the photo button while holding the camera toward the floor. Perhaps that is why the spirit was captured—that picture was never intended to be taken. He may have been caught off guard.

November is Remembrance in Gettysburg because of the anniversary of Lincoln's Gettysburg Address. Luminaries light the graves of Civil War soldiers, and names are read aloud in the night to honor them. As the names were being read, this brilliant cross appeared next to the full moon in the sky over the cemetery.

Spirit Animals and Totems

I began this book writing about Apache Tears, my eight-year-old Sheltie who died just weeks after my first book was published. Her death was unexpected. I rescue old, elderly male dogs. She was my eight-year-old girl. Cancer took her away from my side too soon.

Only a week or so after her passing, my daughter took a trip to South Carolina. She visited a cemetery there and took some photographs. In one of the photographs, unusual light anomalies appeared. At first, I didn't notice her. Then, she was all I could see. In one of the photographs was the exact likeness of my Apache Tears. She was there to give me a

message that she was all right. She was an exceptionally fearful dog during life; I worried about her peaceful crossing in death. She came back to comfort my worries and tell me she is at peace. I do not know how clear the photograph carries over in the book printing process, but she is clear as day in the picture.

Many times, people will send me pictures that have a distinct likeness of their crossed-over pet in the background. I have seen too many of these to classify them as wishful thinking. There are messages being delivered all the time to us; whether we choose to receive them is up to us.

In addition to our beloved spirit pets, each of us has an animal totem, a spirit guardian who walks by us. Ancient people have always believed in the power of totem animals. Totems may come for a brief time to ease our journey, but each of us has a lifelong companion who remains by our side to guide and teach us. I wrote of one paranormal encounter with a totem in my previous book, a black spirit cat that came to comfort me at the time of my young niece's passing.

Starting in early childhood, there is usually one animal to which a person may be especially drawn. Pages of coloring books may be filled with this animal, storybooks may tell of adventures, stuffed replicas may sit as sentries on bedside shelves.

You may find yourself drawn to different totems at different times throughout your life. Several years ago, I kept dreaming of elephants. I kept purchasing little figurines and books. I have always loved elephants; they possess such empathic and sensitive souls. But something very intense was sending me a message during this time concerning the role a pachyderm would play in my life. During this time, my son-in-law was involved in a very serious accident. The day after the accident, my husband and I drove to the scene and walked among the broken bits of wreckage in the road. My downcast eyes looked up above my head, and staring me in the face was a sign with a very large elephant. Now I understood; my elephant totem had been sending me a message. Somehow, I knew he had been watching over that exact spot, a guardian angel with leathered skin and soulful eyes.

Totems come in all sizes. Powerful totems can be tiny; spiders and turtles can bring messages as strong as elephants. To this day, hawks follow me. They circle the Gettysburg sky. I have had them visit in my yard and place of work, perching in the tree outside my window. Once, when traveling the busy avenue of my hometown, a hawk swooped down directly in front of my windshield. It was a startling moment, to have such close contact in such an unexpected place. Yes, hawks follow me; they watch over a kindred spirit, as they once did many centuries ago.

My Personal Paranormal Photography Gallery

(Top) Waiting for a bus perhaps? Only thing is, if you look closely at the woman in the foreground, she has no legs. (Photo taken in London) (Bottom) Notice the orb in the upper balcony—perhaps a spirit looking down? (Photo taken at the Grosvenor Hotel in London)

Richard Felix and I investigating Leap Castle. ....note the Orbs on my back.

(Top and Bottom) Orbs captured at Leap Castle, Ireland.

(Top and Middle) Orbs captured on a former slave plantation in South Carolina. (Bottom) Orb captured at Traitor's Gate at the Tower of London.

Part Nine

Messages from the Dead

A Visit from My Mother

We are closest to the spirit world in the dream state and the hypnotic state. While dreaming, many of us are visited by beloved family members. They seek dreams as their doorway through which to deliver messages and offer guidance; that way, daytime realties and skepticism about spirit communication do not block their entrance.

My mother visited me once many years ago. It was during a very troubled time; I needed her. I remember she looked as she did when I was in elementary school. That seems to be the consensus—spirits appear to be around thirty years old to those of us still in the mortal world. She did not speak one word to me, but she led me to a car. She drove; I talked. We drove through desolate scenery with nothing around. I talked and talked and poured my heart out. Finally, we reached what seemed to be a construction site of a very large mall. We entered this mall, and we walked up to an escalator. She stayed at the top. I looked down the escalator and saw my German Shepherd at the bottom waiting for me. My mother told me that I would have to go down to my dog. She could not follow.

That is the last thing I remember of a "dream" I cannot forget. It was so real; she was there. She did not say one word, but she guided me through this troubled time. Many would say it was just a dream. I can only say that I have never experienced one like it before or since. I truly believe that, while I may have been in my bed, my soul was taking a ride with my mom.

A Little Yellow Bird

When my mother died, I was a young mother myself. Money was tight; things I wanted and things I needed comprised two different categories.

For months before her passing, I would see in a catalogue a little yellow bird that chirped. I loved that bird, but he was expensive; the technology was still new back then. Now, these birds are very inexpensive to purchase. I never bought him, and I never told anyone I liked him. It was my secret.

A couple of days after my mother's burial, I went to visit my dad. He told me that my brother had left something for me on the kitchen table. I walked in the kitchen and saw that bird. From then on, my brother always bought me little yellow birds. A stained glass picture for my window followed one year.

Then, my brother became very seriously ill with sepsis in the hospital. My brother and my mom were very close; I know he had to be talking to her. He told me that, suddenly, a balloon wafted into the room and came to his bed. On that balloon was a little yellow bird. We still have that balloon, though crinkled and flattened. It is a message of love.

Little yellow birds have followed me throughout life, usually when I needed a message of reassurance. I remember when we picked out the bed and breakfast for my daughter's wedding. While touring the garden, a little yellow bird suddenly perched in the tree. I knew it was my mother's way of saying, "Yes, this is the right place."

Animals, birds, and butterflies often bring the messages of loved ones. Inanimate objects, like feathers and pennies, are often left at one's feet. There are always messages if we just open our hearts and minds and look for them. Many more stories such as these can be found in my first book.

A Face in the Curtains

I saw my mother's face in the lace curtains of my bedroom this morning. Crystal clear, it was the face in a photograph I have of her when she was a young woman.

I write these words on the anniversary of her mortal death. Her death happened decades before, when she was still in the prime of her life. As each of us faces our own mortality, the definition of youth gets pushed further and further beyond one's younger days it seems.

Was she there, giving me a small message of comfort, or was my mind conjuring an image to accomplish this feat?

In the paranormal field, there is a term for this, actually more than one term—Matrixing or Paredolia. We have all experienced this phenomenon. Who hasn't looked up at the clouds and envisioned all sorts of fantasy creatures and faces drifting by? This phenomenon occurs a lot in Gettysburg. Once, I saw the vivid face of a soldier in a dead tree trunk. It was so clear; even on my camera screen, it stood out so forcefully. When I later viewed the photo on my computer, the face had vanished. Did I see it? I believe so. I wish I could have captured it for longer than a few moments on my camera screen.

Did I see my mom's face this morning? I believe I did. And to her daughter, that is all that matters on this dreary, grey morning. A morning brightened by a face in the curtain lace, before she drifted by.

My Dad's Hello Each Morning

My mom may bring me a yellow bird, but my dad brings me a rooster. Funny how such insignificant things can become such priceless treasures.

My dad has been gone several years. He was a generous man. Each day, mounds and mounds of charity donation letters would come in the mail. He would give a dollar to as many as he could. Sometimes, certain charities got more. The Veterans of War got $10.00—my dad was a World War II veteran. He liked Mother Hale's House, I remember. Also, the Southwest Indian Foundation. We got a lot of fleece blankets from him. Once, they sent him a thank you picture drawn by a little girl at the Reservation school. I didn't have the heart to tell him it was a photocopied drawing. He thought it was so great.

When he grew too ill to write checks, he asked my daughter to compose a letter for him, his own form letter to send back to charities. He apologized for not being able to give anymore; his fingers couldn't hold a pen, his eyes couldn't see well enough to write checks, and his health was failing.

One of his favorite charities was the National Federation of the Blind. As a thank you for his generosity, they once sent him a wristwatch that made an animal sound announcing whatever hour you wished. The random setting was the rooster. That thing crowed and crowed and crowed. My dad had it counted out—18 crows on the hour.

That crow was a thorn in my side throughout the days I spent taking care of him. Cock-a-doodle-do...every morning at 9 a.m. sharp, and every night at 9 p.m. sharp...18 times......

When my father passed away, I looked around the home for a keepsake. My hand and heart immediately knew which one. That wristwatch.

I remember when it came time to change the clocks, my husband reset it. We didn't have an instruction manual, so he couldn't reset the alarm. I awoke the next morning and heard nothing. No rooster hello from my dad. My heart sank.

My husband toyed around with it. In the middle of the night, around 3 a.m, I heard a chicken clucking. This was NOT right. My husband saw the sadness in my eyes over an inexpensive token watch. He tinkered with it until he fixed it. He is never to touch it again.

My dad's watch is on time again.......at 9 a.m., the rooster is crowing for me. I love that sound; a sound that I once hated is now a sound of remembrance I love.

Sometimes, thorns become the roses in life.

Other times, around anniversary dates, alarm clocks will ring when not set. I have had a musical rocking chair play in the middle of the night. CD players will come on, objects will fall from the shelf in the darkness of night. These are all hellos, just like my morning rooster.

"Higher Ground" (A Poem for my Father)

Looking in my father's eyes
The little girl learning to ride a bike

Looking at my father's hands
The big strong hands that held on until
The little girl rode straight into the bushes

Looking in my father's eyes
The terrified girl in the back seat of the car
Swirling flash flood waters rising

Looking at my father's hands
The determined hands that held the steering wheel
Driving straight toward safety at higher ground

Looking in my father's eyes.....
The first time I saw tears in them

The young woman holding onto her mother's folded hands

As she lay inside her satin bed

Before the casket closed

Looking at my father's hands

As he reached into his wallet

And took out a religious token

Carried every day

Asking his daughter to place it beneath

His wife's pillow

 For her journey

Toward Higher Ground

Looking in my father's eyes

Looking at my mother

One final time

To kiss her forehead

Before the casket closed

Looking in my father's eyes

Whitened by cataracts, lids creased and heavy........

Looking at my father's hands

Crooked, arthritic fingers desperately trying to button a shirt

Looking in a daughter's eyes

Now filled with tears

To see her father's frightened eyes

Look to her for help

Reaching for a daughter's hands

To help him not fall down

Looking in a daughter's eyes

Now filled with fear

Heading straight toward those bushes again

No father's hands to lift her up

To higher ground

Remembering the last time

A grieving daughter's eyes

Watched as the casket closed

Over her father's shut eyes

And still folded hands......

On his journey to Higher Ground

A Rose for My Dad

The last months of my dad's life were arduous. He spent many days in a hospital bed, fighting tests, fighting nurses, fighting me. He just wanted to die, at home and on his own terms.

One afternoon, after yet another battle to get him to eat, get him to try to live another day, my family received a little help and encouragement from the spirit of my mom. Staring up from his hospital room

floor was a card. It said it was the Mystical Rose Petal. Under plastic was the dried petal of a rose. On it was the quotation, "The Power from Heaven shall be known through the Roses."

My mother's name is Rose.

A little card, a little petal from a Rose. Sometimes, it is those inexplicable connections with another Realm that cause intense comfort. My dad passed away at home a couple of weeks later with my children and me at his side. I don't know how that card came to his room that afternoon, but I have a feeling the messenger was divine.

Purple Flowers

I had a dream last night that I was walking through the backyard of my childhood home. When I was very little, this was a peaceful spot. We had a trellis where roses climbed, grape vines intertwined, and tiger lilies blossomed.

Then, one day, my father cleared it away to make space for another driveway. Nothing was said. I wonder how my mother felt. She loved tiger lilies.

It was the dead of winter in my dream. The rose trellis was gone and the ground was still sparse, but growing in the dirt were the most fragile and beautiful purple blossoms. All types—low growing plants, tall bushes—each displaying a beautiful purple bloom.

My father was there. I asked him, "Do you see these? How are they growing in the winter?" He looked at them, then at me, and smiled.

Maybe that is Heaven...a place where all regrets long dormant in the cold winter of the soul are covered again in tiny blooms of rebirth.

The Old Ones Were Wise

My family had two metaphysical teachings. One was that energy or blood draws. The meaning of this covered everything great and small, from bumping into your cousin at the supermarket to finding out that an adopted, long-lost sibling has lived on the next block over for the past twenty years.

We were taught that *like* energy would find *like* energy. We knew this before any metaphysical teachings taught us so.

The other rule was that one life could cross in another's place. All I can tell you is that I have lived through this more times than I will write here, but I will share some memories to explain what I mean.

My son-in-law was in a bad accident a few years ago; it could have ended tragically. My daughter spent many days at the hospital trauma center where he was being treated. One night, upon returning home from the hospital, my daughter found Misty, their cat, silent; she had crossed. (Misty had been my son-in-law's beloved cat; she was very close to him and became a part of my daughter's heart, as well, when they married.) Was the timing of Misty's passing a coincidence? Possibly. But I have lived through too many of these "coincidences" in my family to think so. Did a cat so loving of her master sense what had happened and cross in his place? I will let you judge when you have finished reading.

We were always taught by my mom that one life can go for another. My mom, herself, was once admitted to the hospital in serious condition. At the same time, her closest sister lay in a hospital bed, too. She had been in a coma for quite some time at this point. When news came that my aunt had suddenly passed, I knew that she had gone to save my mother. We did not tell my mother until she recovered, but she knew before we said a word.

One more instance concerned my dog Little Guy. If you read my first book, you know how close the two of us were. I had had Little Guy for several years before he became very ill. It did not look good. By then, he was sixteen. I was dreading the worst. I also had a little parrot at the time. That morning, she started acting funny, not her usual self.

By dinnertime, I had placed a casserole dish in the oven. Suddenly, I was startled by a loud burst inside the oven. My casserole dish had exploded, and dinner was now in fragments on the racks and oven floor. Was it a crack in the dish that had weakened?

I got a sudden "knowing" that this was no mere accident. It was a message meant to get my attention in a big way. When I walked into the other room, my little parrot was motionless on the cage floor. I knew.

I know many of you will say coincidence. But I knew. I called my daughter who was also distraught over Little Guy. When I mentioned my parrot, she knew, as well. My Little Guy recovered and lived three more years.

Now, I am not saying that this happens all the time. But, I am saying that it has happened in my family, and it is something in which I truly believe. I do not fully understand it, but I believe. I believe that one life can go for another.

Part Ten

The Magick of Ireland

Spirit Stone

I was away in Ireland when my close friend died. She fought a valiant battle with ALS and succumbed in her sleep on a Thursday evening. Friday morning, I was walking the grounds of Leap Castle, reputed to be the most haunted castle in Ireland.

Leap is touted as being evil, the home of an Elemental, the darkest form of energy. I was a little apprehensive about visiting here, even more so being sensitive to spirit presence. I was worried something sinister would latch onto my energy. I could not have been more wrong.

The energy around Leap was magickal. Fairy forts and blackthorn wishing trees surround the woods. It is a place where one can easily imagine the fairies playing amidst the morning dew.

A gracious family, the Ryans, now calls Leap home. It is a place filled with music, dance, and reverence for the spirits that were there first.

As I walked up the path to Leap, I looked at the ground. Hundreds, no thousands, of tiny stones filled the path. Stones and stone walls and cairns are everywhere in Ireland.

One tiny white stone caught my eye. No exaggeration, it seemed to be smiling at me. I picked it up. The face on this stone was incredible. There were eyes, a nose, an expressive mouth, and ears. I held it for a few moments, debating in my mind whether or not to put it in my pocket. The feeling of peace and happiness that flowed through this stone and into my entire being is hard to describe. I have never felt such complete bliss. It lit up my whole body; that is the only way I can describe it.

I had always read to leave the fairy realm as it is; so, I put down the stone, which was not easy to do. I walked a few steps, knowing, however, that I must have something of this experience. So, I went back and took a photo.

I memorized where the stone lay in my mind and went up the path to meet my husband, who had gone on ahead. I told him to come back and look at something with me. He immediately saw the face. I asked his advice—should I take this stone? My heart desperately wanted to. He let that decision rest with me. My intuition and knowledge of the supernatural told me to let it be. It was filled with peace in the Irish sun and rain, the wind and woods. Bringing it home to my drawer would be a cruelty. There was no decision; the stone would stay.

My husband took several more photos. We tried to be as inconspicuous as possible. Some other travelers thought we had found a four leaf clover. I didn't answer. I didn't want anyone else taking this spirit from its home.

When I came home from Ireland, I learned that my friend Janet had passed away in her sleep on Thursday night. I now understand the peace and serenity that enveloped me on that path. The last thing my friend told me before I left for Ireland was that she wished she were well enough to go with me. Her daughter told me she lost the ability to speak a couple of days before dying.

I believe my friend did go to Ireland. She was there on that path. She was at peace, free of the bondage of ALS.

She had to part ways with me on our paths in life. Our friendship was not a very long one, but it was a very close one until our paths were parted.

I am at peace with my decision to leave the little stone. Its path was in Ireland and beyond, and I could not interfere with its destiny.

My friend came to say goodbye; her energy came to me in that little stone. How, I don't need to know. I just need to believe. And I do.

I always wanted to believe in the Fairy Realm. After my trip to Ireland, I do. There is a magick in the woods, in the trees, in the stones, an unexplainable presence that is hard to describe unless you have walked among the energy.

The Bone of Sligo Abbey

Sligo Abbey is a strange place. You literally walk among the bones.

This is a place of much death; plagues of sickness have left their mark here...and their bones. There are human bones scattered among the ruins. Leg bones, vertebrae...human bones lay littered like leaves. I have never experienced any such thing. I wonder if any have been carried off.

It is thought to be haunted. How could it not be? Bodies not laid to rest might surely wander the ruins.

My husband found a very small bone in a niche in the wall. It was not human. It looked to be of a small animal, probably a cat. He handed it to me, and as I held it in my hand, something very poignant caught my eye. On the end of

the bone was a perfect paw print, etched in the bone. This was meant for me; the message was clear. It was the spirit of the animals giving me a gift that day in Ireland.

My husband asked if I wanted it. Again, like the stone at Leap, my heart said yes, but my intuition said no. I live in Gettysburg. I walk among a place where the tormented spirits of young men, looking for lost limbs, roam the hallowed fields. To me, human and animal life are equal in worth. They both feel, they both love, they both deserve the same compassion, care, and respect after death. If I found a human bone on the fields of Gettysburg, would I take it? No. So taking this bone would be equally wrong.

I wanted the bearer of this gift to be at peace, not wandering among the ruins in search of a missing piece. I placed the tiny bone back in the niche of the wall. I built a tiny stone cairn to shield it from harm and stealing hands. The gift of its visit was enough. It was a gift I could not keep, only a gift to hold in my hand for a few short moments.

Snail shells are everywhere at Sligo. I let them be. In this strange place where bones are littered among the grounds, I hope even little slug spirits find a home to return to. My first pet as a married woman was a little snail. I had a plant terrarium. One day, I found him and carried him home. He had the most beautiful shell. I put him amidst the plants and gave him what I thought would be a little slug's banquet. After a day or two, I brought him back outside. I knew he would be happiest and healthiest there.

I have always had an understanding that some things must be kept where they are, happy and at peace.

* On an interesting footnote to the subject of monasteries: When I was a very small child, I had *visions* or memories of a monastery. Most of my past life visions have been sorrowful, vignettes of imprisonment, torture, war, or punishment.

The monastery vision was one of peace, of bliss. I often experienced it, but as usual, I spoke not a word of it to my parents. Other young kids longed to go to Disneyland, to Coney Island. Me, I longed to visit the monastery. Weird, yes, but I was an unusual kid. My days were spent in the quiet of my bedroom, reading and drawing. I now realize monastic life would have been a perfect fit in my past, and I believe it was this memory that urged me on to this unique destination.

In a child's mind, I thought my parents could take me in the car. I even envisioned the way, past a cemetery by our house. I knew that if we just kept on that road, we would get there. I would get so frustrated that we never kept going on that road. (Road trips weren't part of my family; we just didn't take them. The most adventurous we ever got was our week at my Aunt Angel's house down the shore in Toms River, New Jersey.)

As I got older, as with most of my visions, this one faded away. I realized that if we kept going on that road, past the cemetery, we would make it to the Atlantic Ocean. And perhaps, that is where my peace remained.

Going to Ireland would finally bring me back to ancient ruins of monasteries, all positioned past the cemetery. I had been waiting half a century to finally reach there.

I am an old soul. By these words, I mean I have lived many lives before this one. I know I have been with several of the same souls, just connected in different ways. For all of us reaching the time of final reincarnation, it is a time of spiritual awakening. It is a time of feeling close to the energy from which all of us were created and to which all of us return. That is why this lifetime has returned extraordinary gifts to me. The earth is filled with many such old souls now, many of them embracing the knowledge that energy connects us all.

There is one other unique twist to this story. Those of you who read my first book learned of my unique connection with a wolf hybrid stray. Nowadays, Gregorian chant albums are popular. Back in the seventies, not many people were tuned in to this type of music. But somehow, there was an album in my husband's collection that had a tiny section of chanting. The only time I heard my boy howl was when this music played. Strange? Maybe, in this mysterious Universe, not so strange at all.

Maybe centuries ago, a hooded monk strolled the Abbey in quiet meditation with a wolf-like friend by his side.

As we were leaving Sligo Abbey, my husband picked up a piece of old wood and gave it to me. I see the face of a long-snouted dog, or perhaps one of the wild deer that roam around Ireland. No matter which way I hold it, the face shines through. I did take this home. It was my thank you for leaving the tiny bone in a respectful manner. The spirits of all the animals who had lived and died near Sligo Abbey followed me that day, and this precious token followed me home across the ocean to remind me of their visit.

Leprechaun's Chair

In the green woods of Ireland, mysterious and magickal things await eyes that look along the path. One such magickal thing is a tree stump, carved by nature to resemble a comfortable Leprechaun chair. There is a back to lean against and a small seat to comfort tired bones. No leprechaun was present when I saw this treasure. At night, though, under the moon and stars, without the presence of a traveler's eye or camera, the magick must begin.

May this magick continue undisturbed. It is what makes Ireland such a unique land with such an unmatched energy.

Ghost Box

I recently purchased a ghost box. This is a device that scans radio waves and channel frequencies. You might be familiar with white noise—spirit energy is believed to have an easier time communicating through these transmissions.

I took this ghost box to Ireland and used it at Kilkenny Castle in the room in which I slept. The previous night, I had icy chills and could not sleep. I used the ghost box in the morning to ask if there was any spirit presence in my room. The results were intriguing.

You can hear the audio transmissions on my blog site, "The Roses and Thorns of Life," at Wordpress.com. The first word to come through was Irish, which was quite appropriate. I asked if he was from the North or South, and "North" was given as his answer. Then, after asking where in Ireland, "Belfast" can be heard coming from this piece of equipment.

My conversation with this spirit revealed his name (Daibhi), his mother's name, and the fact that he had died at seventeen years of age. I asked for him to tell me his love's name; he answered, "I can't do that." I asked him about the chills in my room and felt a tingling all over my hand.

Further communication revealed an injury to his hand. When asked about it, the word "pain" came through. Also, the word "dead" was given after asking if it was a battle injury. I heard the word "contact" come through during the session.

As our spirit conversation drew to a close, the word "end" came through on the ghost box. I asked him to tell me something in Gaelic. He had already given me the Gaelic form of David—his name—in our conversation. His mother's name was Colleen. When asked the family name, "Mac" came in.

Finally, I asked him to say goodbye. Poignantly, the last word given was the Gaelic word for goodbye. A feeling of privilege filled me as I told him goodbye, that he was free of harm and judgment and could move on or stay at the castle as he wished.

The words that flowed from this ghost box were just too coincidental to have been random. There seemed to be an intelligence trying to come through. Many other paranormal investigators have had similar experiences using this type of technology.

Please take a few moments in a very quiet environment to listen to the Electronic Voice Phenomenon sessions on my blog page.

One other ghost box session was done at a circle of standing stones outside the castle. You can hear on the audio the intense wind, the rain, and the song of birds. I cannot interpret any words except for one. When asked what the sacred wood of the Druids was, you can hear the word "oak" given in response.

Whatever your thoughts on using this technology in paranormal investigations, you must admit that the answers are intriguing and must not be casually tossed aside as mere changing of the channels.

Respect for the Spirits

One of the most offensive behaviors a human can display is utter disrespect for the paranormal and spiritual realm.

While in Ireland, I was very excited to attend a séance in Ballygally Castle. Ballygally is believed to be haunted by the sad spirit of a young woman who was imprisoned in the tower after giving birth to a child. Some claim that after hearing her baby cry, she broke down her door and fell tragically down a perilous flight of stairs. Others believe she may have jumped or been pushed out of the tower window. (I have seen the tower window. It is highly unlikely that either of these scenarios would have happened due to its dimensions.) It is said that she still wanders the castle in search of her child. I was anxious to try to communicate with her.

The tour director was organizing this séance. Well-known paranormal historian Richard Felix was attending. I arrived before Richard did. The tour director was just about to shut the lights in the séance room.

I feel energy and auras. I walked around the room and came to a spot where I sensed energy's presence. I stood there, against the wall, eager for the night to commence.

As the lights went out, suddenly a sharp blow dug into my back. It seems the tour director had set up a prank, hoping to get a rise out of Richard Felix. Someone was hiding in a little wall closet behind me. I had not seen this, but I sure felt the force of the closet door in my back as the hiding attendee burst forth into the room.

I was utterly disgusted. I left the séance room with a bruised back. Richard Felix never did come that night; he was in pain from an injury he had incurred shortly before the trip.

The saddest thing is that an opportunity to communicate with a tormented spirit was lost. Foolish pranks have no place in the world of paranormal research. They degrade the work that I do, and they offend the Spirit World.

Any attempt at communication that night was lost, which is sad because I had felt spirit presence strongly in this castle as I went upstairs to a little *Ghost Room* (where that young mother may have tragically fallen down the stairs, rushing to her baby's cries). It was a similar physical reaction to the one I felt at the Tillie Pierce House in Gettysburg. I really believe we would have achieved some communication that night had the séance been held in a respectful manner. But I will never know; a foolish prank overshadowed all.

If you wish to connect with the spirit realm, it must be done with reverence and an open mind. Spirits are just like us—they are lonely, trying to reach out to a lost plane of existence in which they can no longer walk freely. Extending a hand in kindness and respect is the only way to achieve connection.

The photo below was taken at the base of the haunted stairway leading up to the Ghost Room at Ballygally Castle. My husband wanted to take a photograph. I refused to sit in this chair; it had an ominous energy about it. I stood beside it instead, not wanting to mingle my energy with whatever presence was in this room. When the photo appeared on his camera, I was not *beside* the chair, but *behind* it. The chair seems to loom largely about me, trying to envelope my energy. It seems my intuition was correct; I was right not to sit in this chair. I call it my "Alice and the Looking Glass Chair."

Part Eleven

Goodbye to a Friend

A Heroine's Poppy

When I returned home from Ireland, Janet visited me again from the spirit realm.

My plane landed on Sunday. Her memorial service was the next day. Upon arriving in Gettysburg for her service, I walked the path to my farmhouse door, passing by the small patch of poppies growing in my garden. The year before, Janet had told me how much she liked poppies and how sorry she was that she had pulled out some in her own garden.

That morning, the morning of the service, all of my poppies were just growing green buds and a long way from opening........except one.  One poppy stood tall and opened fully to the world, smiling its big red smile as I walked past.

This was Janet, a heroine. She fought a war with ALS. It was a war which ravaged her strength, but not her spirit, her humor, or her grace. She kept those until her last day.

Poppies are for fallen heroes. Thank you, Janet, for saying, "Hello, I am still around." You are my hero. Whenever I had a crummy day and started to complain, I thought of you. How you could not use your hands to write, to knit, to play the ukulele I gave you for your birthday. ALS did not defeat your spirit; it lives on and will be remembered by me as long as I walk this earth. And one day, we will walk the Universe as mateys again.

At the beginning of my book, you might have read my dedication page to JBee, my friend. This is Janet. I called her JBee because she loved bees. She had just started to raise her own but had to stop when ALS struck.

Before she died, Janet gave me a hand-sewn apron she had made with sunflowers and bees on it. She had once written that on unhappy days, she would put on a happy apron and bake something; then, those days would be better.

JBee, I wish putting on that apron could make these days of grief better...but a small piece of hand-sewn cloth will surround me with the comfort of a friend.

Part Twelve

From a Place of War to a Place of Wonder

This Magical Place

Gettysburg is a magical place. Once you visit, some magical spell invades your skin and enters your blood. A longing compels you to come back again and again. It compelled me so much so that I purchased a farmhouse there.

The very first time my husband and I visited Gettysburg, we encountered a horrific storm on the way. This was a monster of a storm; the sky looked as if a bicycle-riding witch would pass by any moment. Our vehicle was being battered by wind and intense rain. Visibility was next to nothing. Halfway there, I wanted to turn back. I feared this was an omen telling me to stay away, but we continued. I always had an intense knowing that Gettysburg had some importance to me.....now it was as if this storm was testing my will to get there and find it.

But get there we did, and the Gettysburg sun had come out by the time we reached our Inn. We checked our bags, walked outside, and lo and behold, a beautiful rainbow appeared on the horizon. It was the sign of home....I was Dorothy, finding my way back to a place I feel I have walked on before...in another kind of storm.

That storm happened at precisely the half-way point of our first drive out to Gettysburg. Now, each time I drive out there, I always know when we are exactly half the distance between our two homes.

I truly believe that those of us compelled to return to these rolling hills have been here before. We have battled, nursed, or witnessed such horror that our souls are imprinted with indelible marks. Talk to those who honor these grounds—the reenactors, the battlefield guides, those who make the trek yearly and would rather spend a week in Gettysburg than on some tropical beach—and you will see a common thread evolve, the thread that links us all here—the knowledge that we have walked here before, walked among the fallen, the wounded, the traumatized survivors of several sweltering July days in 1863 and beyond. We now find peace, walking among the ghosts.

Even those who visit Gettysburg only once do not leave without some unexplainable experience or impression on their hearts. I hope that the wandering souls have built their own village of sorts, of love, of comradeship, of peace. Perhaps the lost and wandering wish to be remembered, wish to be visited, wish to feel their deaths are still respected today. If you are fortunate to be one of the chosen who encounters a wandering soul, tell him this is true. Tell him we will continue to honor and watch over the hallowed grounds on which his spirit (and others) roams.

Though dead, this tree on the battlefield in Gettysburg still carries such an energy-filled presence.

But you don't have to travel to Gettysburg to encounter the paranormal. Spirit energy is around us everywhere. It walks by our sides in daylight, and it enters our dreams at night. I hope this book has opened your eyes and hearts to this belief. We are all energy just going through existence on a different plane or wrinkle in time.

Someday, all of those wrinkles will be ironed out, and people will understand, not fear.

Rainbows on Both Sides of the World

Yes, rainbows have always welcomed this Dorothy home to Pennsylvania's Hallowed Grounds, along with the scarecrow on my farmhouse land that dons my father's plaid shirt.

I don't believe that my stormy past lives skipped visiting the Emerald Isle. Perhaps that is why so many

rainbows met me on my visit to Ireland. They don't herald a leprechaun's pot of gold; to me, they symbolize a welcoming home from the sky.

Through persecutions, through battles, through whatever the

past brought to my door, I know a rainbow was waiting after each storm. Through storms in life, there will always be rainbows to comfort if

you turn your eyes toward the stars and sky.

Watching a Butterfly Fall Asleep

L ast summer at my farmhouse, I sat at my window near the close of day and witnessed one of the most magical moments in my life. I will always remember it. I watched a Monarch butterfly flutter by.

He drifted among the branches of my tree, leaf to leaf, inspecting each potential bed, his wings rapidly moving through the air.

Then, suddenly, he stopped at one spot high in the branches. The fluttering of his wings slowly grew more and more peaceful until finally, his wings clasped shut (as if in prayer) as he hung upside down.

I had watched him fall asleep.

I felt so honored that he chose my tree as his sanctuary for the night...and so special to be witness to the last moments of a busy day of flight.

We all have busy days of flight—hurrying from branch to branch and leaf to leaf. So much of these days flutter into our nights and make it hard for us to clasp our minds in peace and solitude and drift to sleep...

Such a tiny little creature, with the fortitude to travel across the continent to search for rest, found it for the night in my tree. I felt so blessed to have seen this magical moment.

Sometimes, when the stress and hurry of my life becomes overwhelming, I think upon that tiny Monarch butterfly, cradled in leaves of peace outside my window.

The hustle and bustle has left a blindness in our third eye, the part of our being opened to the supernatural and paranormal. Coming back to earth and nature can illuminate that blind spot again.

The doorway is there waiting. Once opened, a universe of mysteries unfolds before the soul. Sometimes, a tiny being like a butterfly can help us find the key.

My Work with Animals

There are certain moments that shape a life...all it takes is a moment for the eyes and heart to register a memory, a sadness, a lingering image that haunts the mind from youth to death. These moments change a life; they forge a path and set an intention and purpose to one's momentary existence on this earth.

One such moment happened to me when I was very little. My aunt had a beach house on the Jersey shore. We would spend a week there, at Lake Riviera, each summer. One summer day, returning home from the lake, I saw a toad by the side of the sandy, wooded path. He seemed sick; something wasn't right. Most little girls would have run as fast as their legs permitted, but I scooped him up. I remember his skin oozing a substance into the palms of my hands. I don't think my mother was too thrilled, but she let me take him home.

I put him in the yard to convalesce. I don't remember what I fed him, but I am certain it wasn't a proper toad diet. He didn't get better. Afraid I was doing more harm than good, I brought him back to that path again and put him in a safe spot—or so I thought.

The next day, while headed to the lake with my mother, I saw a group of young teens playing volleyball on the beach. Only they weren't using a ball—they were using a toad. That moment was branded into my being. Perhaps that was the moment I decided to save them all, or at least a few…….

All it takes is one moment, one step on that path to change a life—both a toad's and a girl's.

A Comforting Goodbye

I began my story with death, and now I'll end my story with death because as one life ends, another begins. There are no endings, only beginnings to which we must open our minds and hearts.

Another sad day. My old and gentle dwarf bunny, Mossflower, was laid to rest in the farm garden.

I always had a bunny. There are so many varieties now—some with upright ears, some with lopped ones. I am partial to the little brown ones that look as if they hopped right out of a woodland forest. Mossflower, or Mossie as I called her, was one such bunny. Some might have thought her to be plain; I thought she was beautiful.

She lived longer than a little dwarf bunny is expected to live, but losing her was not any easier because of this.

We had just laid her to rest as it was getting dark. I was about to leave and head back to my New Jersey home. Before doing so, I stopped at her grave to say goodbye. I told her I hoped she was happy where we placed her and not to feel frightened or alone.

As I walked from her grave to the front path of my farmhouse, a little brown bunny hopped in front of my feet and dashed into the fields beyond. A little bunny just like my Mossie, out of the woodlands...

Was it Mossie? Was it a sign from her that she was fine? Or did a little brown bunny choose a perfect time to say hello? Whichever you may believe, I can tell you it made my grieving heart sing.

Epilogue

I found the perfect remembrance keepsake for my young grandson. Those of you who have followed by blogs might remember one I wrote a couple of days after he was born. In it, I called my heart a compass with an arrow that now pointed directly to him.

I found that compass in a Civil War artifacts shop a couple of days before writing that blog. At a time when my spirit no longer dwells on earth, it (along with my words) will remind him still of his grandma's constant heart.

Writers let a little of their hearts seep out into their work; each blog or story lets readers peer into tiny cracks in the walls of their hearts. In the words—sometimes, more so between the words—secrets may be revealed.

Each page I write, I leave behind a snippet of myself for my grandson and perhaps others who may follow. I lost another grandchild before her spirit reached the earth; her heart stopped beating. But her tiny heart still beats within mine—and will continue to do so until our energies one day unite.

My dad wrote one letter each day for almost twenty years to my mother after she died. The ravages of arthritis took his ability to write several years before his own death; his once beautiful penmanship was destroyed by mortality's foe. Before he died, he asked me if anyone would like his letters. I could not ask for them. I know they revealed too many cracks and secrets of his heart. I thought it best he make the decision of their fate. He told me one morning he had shredded them.

I wanted those letters more than anything, but they were not mine to own. A writer must decide what he/she wishes readers to own.

He left me one page of his letters, the last one, in which he told my mom his fingers could not hold the pen and write anymore.

One day, that page will pass on to his grandchildren and mine.

One day, the pages of my books and life will pass on as well, letting those who never knew me look inside the cracks of my own heart.

Until then, my heart compass will always point to the ones I love. And one day, those who carry a snippet of my own energy will continue to peer into the cracks of my heart through each word left on my pages.

"I Am a Winter Soul"

I look forward to October

It heralds in Winter

I am a Winter Soul

I think most writers are.

The quiet introvert

No butterfly wings of the party Summer

Adorn my Winter form.

Dark hair, fair skin

A "Winter" in fashion magazines

And Winter in my soul

I seek...

Staying in

Inside my intuition

Inside my shelter

Winter snows are cleansing

Dirty streets are washed clean

For a time

Give me a quiet snow

To Shroud

My contemplative Soul

Not sunlight's glare on a crowded beach

To overwhelm and burn

For I am

A Winter Soul...

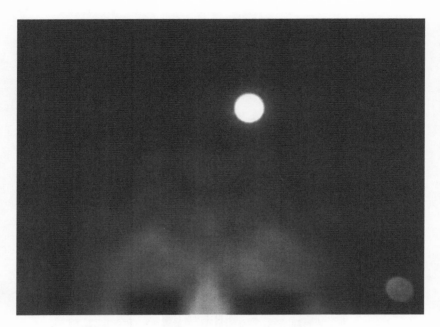

Under a full moon, an angel seems to be rising. Note also the little orb to her right. Maybe she is bringing a newly departed soul home. (Photo taken at Green-wood Cemetery, Brooklyn, New York)

Made in the USA
San Bernardino, CA
24 November 2014